REALISTS
AND NOMINALISTS

REALISTS
AND NOMINALISTS

MEYRICK H. CARRÉ
Lecturer in Philosophy, University of Bristol

OXFORD UNIVERSITY PRESS

Oxford University Press, Ely House, London W. 1

GLASGOW   NEW YORK   TORONTO   MELBOURNE   WELLINGTON
CAPE TOWN   SALISBURY   IBADAN   NAIROBI   LUSAKA   ADDIS ABABA
BOMBAY   CALCUTTA   MADRAS   KARACHI   LAHORE   DACCA
KUALA LUMPUR   HONG KONG   TOKYO

FIRST PUBLISHED MARCH 1946
SECOND IMPRESSION OCTOBER 1946
REPRINTED LITHOGRAPHICALLY IN GREAT BRITAIN
AT THE UNIVERSITY PRESS, OXFORD
FROM SHEETS OF THE SECOND IMPRESSION, 1950, 1961, 1967

PREFACE

THE brief studies that follow are intended to be an introduction to some of the great stages of thought that lie between the disruption of the Roman Empire in the West and the period of the Renaissance. I am well aware that the passages that have been selected for discussion are mere fractions torn from a vast and intricate history, but I hope they will serve some inquirers who wish to reconnoitre the frontiers of a new country. Students of philosophy are still apt to flit from the theories of classical Greece to the scientific assumptions of the seventeenth century without bestowing more than a hasty glance at the intervening eras of speculation. To say the least, this is an unhistorical procedure. The bond that unites the ancient outlook with the new is the persistence of Greek principles within the context of Christian doctrine. And the new conceptions, despite their loud rejection of Scholasticism, were deeply indebted to the medieval methods and are inexplicable without some appreciation of them.

Philosophers of the modern era concentrated their attention upon problems relating to the scope and validity of human knowledge. Such questions were assuredly not the primary concern of medieval thinkers. Yet in their immense and subtle inquiries into the rational order of existence they were necessarily led to investigate the nature of reason. It is this aspect of medieval thought that I have selected for description here. Although this approach is not the normal path to the understanding of the great scholastics, it allows the student to compare their treatment of questions that became prominent in later thought with modern discussions of these questions. And this aspect of Latin Christian philosophy brings us into touch with one of the central debates of the medieval era, the dispute over the status of general ideas, or universals.

In a limited survey simplification is inevitable. But instead of attempting to range over the vast field in a general manner I have sought to bring the reader close to the method and quality of scholastic argument by collecting the opinions of four representative figures. St. Augustine exercised a cardinal influence on all speculation from the earliest to the latest phase of medieval thought. From him, more than from any other authority, sprang the pronounced Realism that persisted into modern times. In the eleventh century there appeared a new view of knowledge that conflicted with the spiritual theory of Augustine and with his Neo-Platonic Realism. The first and most formidable critic of the older tradition was Peter Abaelard, and I have tried to show the substance of his attack on extreme Realism by following closely the argument of one of his works. The next great stage occurred in the thirteenth century, when St. Thomas Aquinas forged a new doctrine of experience founded upon an independent examination of the text of Aristotle, now for the first time made available in its authentic character. His theory of knowledge sought to combine the merits of the older and the newer outlooks, and his carefully balanced Realism united the claims of both the general and particular constituents of experience. But the fourteenth century saw novel and audacious theories in philosophy. One mark of the collapse of the great tradition was the appearance of Nominalism. The champion of this radical departure was William of Ockham. In him medieval reflection discovered its Hume. With him our brief illustrations of medieval accounts of knowledge must end.

Guided by recent expositors I have gone as far as I was able to the texts of my authorities. In the case of William of Ockham I have been compelled to rely on the copious quotations from his writings in the works of Abbagnano and of Tornay; for there are no modern editions of his main treatises. A list of books to which I am especially indebted is given at the end of the volume. There is one pre-eminent writer on medieval philosophy to whom every student must be gratefully obliged, whatever part of the field he explores, namely, Professor Etienne Gilson. At every point I have been aided by his incomparable learning and brilliant expositions. Professor C. C. J. Webb kindly read an early draft of the chapter on St. Augustine and sent me some instructive comments. The book was completed before the war; it has been revised, so far as circumstances permitted, during the war.

M. H. C.

CONTENTS

I

ST. AUGUSTINE

I

AUGUSTINE was born in the year 354 at Tagaste, a small town in the Roman province of Numidia in north Africa. His father, Patricius, held an official position in the town; he died when Augustine was seventeen years old. His mother, Monica, was a devout Christian, who exercised a profound influence on her extraordinary son. As a boy Augustine showed striking, though wayward, abilities, and at an early age was sent to continue his studies at the University of Carthage. Here he distinguished himself in rhetoric, though his fervent nature and the frivolity of student life in Carthage often led him into dissipation. Carthage was a centre of Manichæism, a creed which incongruously combined doctrines drawn from Christianity and Zoroastrianism, and Augustine became for many years an adherent of the sect. A reading in his nineteenth year of a book by Cicero, *Hortensius*, kindled a passionate interest in philosophy. Upon the completion of his University course he taught rhetoric at Carthage. In the year 384, following a brief visit to Rome, he was elected to a professorship at Milan. Throughout these years at Carthage and Milan Augustine suffered

ABBREVIATIONS

C.S.E.L.	Corpus Scriptorum Ecclesiasticorum Latinorum. The figures refer to the volume and page.
P.L.	Patrologia Latina, edited Migne. The figures refer to the volume and column.
Confess.	Confessionum libri tredecim. The edition used is that edited by Gibb and Montgomery, Cambridge, 1927.
Contra Acad.	Contra Academicos.
De an.	De anima et ejus origine.
De civ. Dei	De civitate Dei.
De divers. Quaest.	De diversis quaestionibus octoginta tribus.
De Gen. ad litt.	De Genesi ad litteram.
De lib. arb.	De libero arbitrio.
De mag.	De magistro.
De mus.	De musica.
De ord.	De ordine.
De quant. an.	De quantitate animae.
De Trin.	De Trinitate.
De vera rel.	De vera religione.
Ep.	Epistolae.
Serm.	Sermones.
Solil.	Soliloquia.

acute mental conflict. He became increasingly dissatisfied with the tenets of the Manichees. The doctrines of Christianity deeply attracted him, but he found himself unable wholly to embrace its creed. Persistently he sought to free himself from the materialist theory of reality which he had learnt from the Manichæan philosophers.

'If I had been able to conceive a spiritual substance, all their specious arguments would have been destroyed at one blow, and cast out of my mind; but I could not. Yet so far as concerned the physical aspect of this world and the entire realm of nature apprehended by the bodily senses, I came to the conclusion, the further I gave myself to reflection and comparison, that the tenets of most of the philosophers were far more acceptable. Consequently, in the manner of the Academic School, as it is usually interpreted, doubting everything and wavering between all, I made up my mind to abandon the Manichees. For I felt that while I remained in a state of doubt I ought not to continue to belong to a sect to which I already preferred certain philosophers. Yet to these philosophers since they were without the saving name of Christ, I utterly refused to entrust the care of my sick soul.'[1]

The philosophers to whom he owed his liberation were the Platonists. Through the study of them he was led to accept as rationally legitimate an order of reality beyond the material world, an order for which his soul craved. The influence of these philosophers coincides with profound personal experience. The further steps in his conversion to the Christian Faith—the sermons of Ambrose, the conversation with Simplician, the scene in the garden —are touchingly described in the *Confessions*. He resigned his professorship and retired with a few intimate friends to a villa at Cassiacum in the neighbourhood of Milan. In the books written at this time, *Against the Academic Philosophers, On Order*, and *On the Blessed Life*, Augustine gives a charming picture of the little group of disciples who had gathered round him. He records the eager study of the classics; the long evening discussions under the spreading tree in the meadow; his own solitary vigils to the murmur of the little stream outside his room.

Shortly after his baptism, when the party were preparing to return to Africa, Augustine was overwhelmed with grief by the death of Monica. He returned to Rome and, in 388, to Africa. There at his native town of Tagaste he lived the life of an ascetic. To this period, from 386 to 391, belong the works which contain

---

[1] Confess. v. xiv. 25.

a large measure of his philosophical teaching, the treatises *On the Immortality of the Soul, On Music, On the Extensity of the Soul,* and *On Free Will.* His conversion marked not only a moral and religious change; it was also a turning away from literature and rhetoric to philosophy and theology. The first series of treatises directed against the doctrines of the Manichæans appeared also at this time. In his forty-first year, such was his reputation in the Christian community, he was consecrated Bishop.

For thirty-five years Augustine gave himself unremittingly to the welfare of his diocese, and far beyond its bounds dominated the councils of the Church in Africa. But in spite of his ecclesiastical care, in spite of ill health, he continued to pour out a vast range of works. He engaged the sects which threatened the Church, the Manichees, the Donatists, the Pelagians, the Arians, in detailed and tireless controversy. These controversial books alone number forty-four. He published fifteen commentaries on the Scriptures. Of his other writings two have made a general appeal throughout the ages. *The Confessions* were composed in order to check the flattery which was directed by Christians everywhere in the Empire towards the great Bishop. They contain a pathetic revelation of his early struggles for peace of mind, and disclose the humility of a saint. *The City of God* is a huge work upon which Augustine was engaged for fourteen years. In it he contrasts at length the kingdom of God with the secular state, describes the evolution of humanity, and ranges over the system of Christian beliefs. Of his other numerous works, those *On the Master* (a discussion on the principles of teaching), *On the Trinity,* and *On the Literal Interpretation of Genesis* include passages which are of philosophical interest.

The latter years of Augustine witnessed the ruin of the civilized world. The barbarians streamed through the defences of the Empire. Soon their hordes were devastating Italy. Armies revolted; usurpers appeared. Finally in 410 men heard with despair that the Eternal City had fallen. Africa was filled with fugitives from Rome. The broken Empire was further shattered by intrigues. At length the doom fell upon the African provinces. Boniface, Count of Africa, invited the Vandals to support his cause. Swiftly the Roman districts were overrun. Boniface was soon in flight before his recent allies and the remnants of his force were penned in Hippo. These disasters embittered the last days of Augustine.

Three months after the beginning of the siege he fell ill, and at the end of August in the year 430 he died. A year later Hippo was captured and given to the flames.

The vast intellectual activity of Augustine must be appreciated against the culture of the period. It was an age in which the standards of learning were in process of decay. Scientific and philosophical reflection had begun to wane before the Christian era, and the later phases of the Roman Empire saw a further decline in the standards and range of inquiry. What survived of Greek thought became suffused with morality and with theology. The mind of the Roman was practical and political, and Cicero praises his countrymen because, thanks to the gods, they were not like the Greeks, and knew how to limit the study of mathematics to useful purposes.[1] The compendia of natural knowledge that provided men with the science of the physical world were haphazard collections of curiosities and superstitions. There was little attempt to verify the tales handed down by tradition or to seek a coherent explanation of the facts. The guiding influence on Roman education was oratory. But even this was studied in an artificial and mechanical style. In the schools the attention of the pupils was concentrated upon formal rules of grammar and syntax and they were trained to classify topics in superficial divisions and subdivisions. The literary masterpieces of the past were dissected with little appreciation of their spirit. This pedantic education deeply affected thought, and its consequences can be noticed in the writings of Augustine. He is fond of verbal distinctions. The argument is often lacking in rigour, it rambles and loses sight of the point at issue. He had received the best education that his time could offer, but his knowledge of Greek is scanty, and he cites the Greek philosophers in Latin translations. Jerome remarks that hardly anyone in his day was reading Aristotle and few had heard so much as the name of Plato. This is exaggeration. But Augustine complains that his fellow students at Carthage could make nothing of Aristotle's *Categories*, in spite of the eloquence of their masters.[2] In reading Augustine it must not be forgotten that his training was in the school not of Greek philosophy, but of Cicero.[3]

Yet he did more than any other Christian teacher to bring Christian conceptions into touch with philosophical principles.

---

[1] *Tusculanae*, i. 2.   [2] Confess. IV. xvi. 28.
[3] H. I. Marrou, *St. Augustin et la fin de la Culture Antique*, Paris, 1938, investigates in detail Augustine's attainments.

Hostility to learning was general in the Church. 'The common herd', wrote Clement of Alexandria, of his flock, 'fear Greek philosophy as children fear goblins.' Nor was it only the common herd who rejected the heritage of thought in favour of simple faith. Some of the leaders were vehemently opposed to speculation. For Tertullian all the teaching of secular literature is foolishness and a Christian must ignore it. Philosophers make a trade of notoriety and set out to destroy virtue.[1] And dialectic, the invention of 'the wretched Aristotle', is the mother of heresy. 'Let those who profess a Christianity affected by the Stoic, Platonic, or Dialectical philosophy beware. We ourselves have no need for curiosity after Jesus Christ, nor for investigation, after the Gospel.'[2] Even Augustine's master, Ambrose, looked on philosophy with suspicion and asserted that all that was good in the Greeks had been borrowed from Scripture. The Faith gives men all that is necessary to know.

The searching and comprehensive inquiries of Augustine led the meditations of subsequent generations of churchmen to pass beyond this rule of pious ignorance. His writings invited men to examine the rational basis of their faith. He did not deny that it is necessary to believe in order to know; understanding is the reward of faith. But he declared also that Christian doctrine contains many things that we cannot believe unless we understand them. A man who thinks it is sufficient to hold fast to the Faith without aspiring to an understanding of it ignores the true end of faith.[3] No man of his age was better fitted to provide Christian beliefs with a metaphysical foundation. He had passed through the ferment of Oriental theosophy. He had wrestled with scepticism. He was steeped in the tenets of the most profound philosophy of his time. His speculations are stamped with the mark of his studies in Neoplatonism. The thinkers he cites in *De civitate Dei* as those to whom he owed his intellectual salvation are Plotinus, Jamblichus, Porphyry, and Apuleius. There is much, indeed, in Plotinus that he found lacking, and there were cardinal points in the system of the *Enneads* that he rejected. But it is principally through Augustine that the Hellenic tradition of thought was united with Western Catholic philosophy and theology. He adapted and inserted into a Christian context the Neoplatonic conceptions of reality. The low state of culture of his era affected his philosophical discussions. But his intellectual diligence was unparalleled; and he was endowed

---

[1] *Apologeticum*, 46.   [2] *De Praescriptionibus Haereticorum*, 7.
[3] Ep. cxx.

with a disposition 'that longed not merely to believe the truth, but also to understand it'.[1]

His philosophical views as a whole are nowhere coherently set forth. At an early age of his career, as we have seen, his ethical and metaphysical inquiries were thrown aside for pressing doctrinal controversies. Discussions of purely philosophical interest are henceforth to be found embedded in the theological and exegetical treatises. They are scattered widely through the enormous compass of Augustine's works. But in truth this division between the philosophical and theological aspects of his thought is foreign to Augustine's intentions. Philosophy for him is intrinsically joined with theology. 'I desire to know God and the soul. Nothing besides? Nothing at all.'[2] The end of philosophy is not knowledge but wisdom. Knowledge is concerned with temporal events. Its field is, as we should say, science. Wisdom is the apprehension of eternal things. And wisdom is a part of the blessed life.[3]

Accordingly we do not find in Augustine the distinction between the realm of Reason and the realm of Faith which is seen in later scholastic writers. He reserves, indeed, certain spheres wherein Faith precedes Reason, namely those dogmas of the Christian religion which pertain to salvation.[4] Faith does not here exclude Reason. It is Reason informed with religious perception. 'Far be it', he says, 'that we should have faith without accepting or demanding reason for our faith.'[5] And he adds that faith is only possible to rational beings. But he held, too, that failure to understand the truths of faith is to be ascribed not wholly to intellectual defect, but also to moral obliquity.[6]

In spite, however, of the organic relation of philosophical discussions to the theological expositions in which they are set, a series of arguments concerning the nature and validity of knowledge that form a consistent scheme of metaphysical thought, may be detached from the writings of the great Bishop. His examination of the principles of thought are part of a vast proof for the existence of God; though from this aspect God is to be conceived as the ideal of knowledge implicit in all human endeavour after understanding, the ideal of an all-embracing coherent unity of experience.

We may now venture to describe, as closely as possible in his own terms, Augustine's theory of knowledge.

[1] Contra Acad. III. xx. 43; C.S.E.L. lxiii. 80.   [2] Solil. I. ii. 7; P.L. xxxii. 872.
[2] De Trin. XII. xv. 25; P.L. xlii. 1018.   [4] Ep. cxx. i. 3; C.S.E.L. xxxiv. 706.
[3] Ib.   [6] De Trin. xv. xxvii. 50; P.L. xlii. 1097.

II

In a passage in the *Confessions* Augustine gives an epitome of his doctrine.

'And thus by degrees I passed from bodies to the bodily sensations of the mind. And from this stage I came next to the mind's inner faculty, to which the bodily senses refer external objects. And this is the limit of the intelligence of animals. Passing beyond this I proceeded next to the rational faculty to which all that is collected from the bodily senses is referred for judgement. And this faculty perceiving itself in me also to be unstable raised itself to its intellectual level, and turned the mind's reflections away from the tyranny of habit, withdrawing itself from the throngs of confusing images, in order that it might find the light by which it was suffused. For with complete conviction it proclaimed that what is unchangeable is to be preferred to what is changeable, and thus it had knowledge of the unchangeable itself. For unless it had in some way known to it, the mind would have had no ground for preferring it to the changeable. And so in one tremulous stroke of vision it arrived at that which is.'[1]

Bodies, sensation, inner sense, judgement, pure thought, intuition—such are the steps in Augustine's investigation of knowledge.[2] The prevailing purpose of the investigation is to prove the existence of a realm of absolute timeless reality. Each grade of knowledge is shown to rest on a more stable, more comprehensive, more fundamental mode of cognition. The chief defect which compels the mind to press on from the earlier to the later forms of apprehension, from the knowledge of physical objects to the contemplation of the Ideas, is the presence of impermanence. The intellect perceives above the flux of visible things and above human minds a system of unchangeable truths.[3] And the *res intelligibles* which are open to the grasp of intellectual insight are not merely formal propositions; they are the constitutive principles of things. Endowed with the power of 'illumination' the mind may descry beyond space and time the source of Ideas.

Augustine recurs to this ascent towards reality in many different forms. In a notable passage in *De quantitate animae*[4] seven steps of

---

[1] Confess. VII. xvii. 23.

[2] For Augustine thought (*mens*) embraces both reason (*ratio*) and intellectual understanding (*intellectus*). Reason is the distinctively human power of discovering relevant connexions by a process of analysis and synthesis. *Intellectus* apprehends those infallible truths which are clues to the nature of reality. In the exercise of this faculty man attains to some knowledge of purely spiritual substances. [3] De divers. Quaest. xlv. 1; P.L. xl. 28.

[4] Op. cit. xxxiii. 70 ff.; P.L. xxxii. 1073.

mental development are distinguished. In the first stage the mind appears, even in plants, as life preserving the unity of the physical structure and causing growth and reproduction. At the next level it perceives through the senses and exhibits the primary animal appetites. Next it shows itself in man as tradition and custom. Fourthly, the mind rises above the interests of the external world to the region of moral life. Next it reaches a state of joyful confidence and proceeds to the sixth stage, in which it strives to understand those things which truly and supremely exist. Finally it attains a vision of truth.

Often the movement of his thought is more direct. The human mind in considering visible things can recognize that it is itself superior to them. But since it falls short of wisdom and is still trying to reach it, it becomes aware that its own nature is transient and perceives beyond itself the unchanging truth.[1]

In the course of his numerous explorations of this ascent of the mind Augustine necessarily discusses the elements of which knowledge is composed. He analyses mental processes such as perception and judgement so as to exhibit the complex activities present in them. His views on these points, especially the account of the relation between physical impressions and sensations, profoundly affected the philosophy of the Middle Ages. But it is important to realize that psychological analysis is incidental to Augustine's main concern. He is preoccupied with the nature of reality which he finds disclosed in the spirit's search for truth. It is the metaphysical question concerning the status of various types of knowledge which interests him. He passes over, as we shall notice, important points in the psychology of knowledge in order to press the mind's recognition of the Ideas.

A further characteristic, which introduces the distinctive approach of medieval thought to these topics, must be mentioned. Throughout Augustine's discussions of logical and psychological questions an intimate relation with moral notions is maintained. The higher mental activity, for example, is also the better.

'*Augustine.* Now to which of these three belongs all that the bodily sense perceives? . . . is it to be placed in that class which only exists or in that which also lives, or in that which also understands? *Evodius.* In that which only exists. *A.* Then in which class of these three do you suppose sense itself to fall? *E.* In that which lives. *A.* Which of these two then do you judge to be better? Sense itself or that which sense

---

[1] Cf. De divers. Quaest., passage cited above.

perceives? *E*. Sense, surely. *A*. Why? *E*. Because that which also lives is better than that which only exists.'[1]

The discussion is transferred from a classification in point of natural order to a classification in point of value. Always the discussions on knowledge press the moral superiority of one mode of experience over another. Mind is nobler than the body, reason higher than sense. The quest for the Ideas is the quest for spiritual value.

To detach from this concentration on truth conceived as a way to blessedness and salvation discussions of theoretical import offers some violence to Augustine's thought. As M. Gilson observes, it is difficult at any point to say with precision 'whether Saint Augustine is speaking as a theologian or as a philosopher, whether he is proving the existence of God or developing a theory of knowledge, whether the eternal truths of which he speaks are those of under-standing or of morality, whether it is a doctrine of sensation which he is expounding or the consequences of original Sin'.[2] The rejec-tion of the sensible order is a facet of the condemnation of the flesh. The independence of mind and body and the supremacy of the eternal Ideas are aspects of the ascendancy of spirit over matter.

With these considerations in mind let us now turn to the first stages of the mind's ascent to truth.

III

We have seen that a crucial stage in the development of Augustine's mind was the discovery of a reply to the challenge which the fashionable school of philosophy had brought against the validity of knowledge. The thought of the age was widely influenced by the tradition of Pyrrho, according to which all our knowledge is infected with subjectivity. The real nature of things is wholly unknown to us. Since nothing is certain, a suspension of judgement is the only prudent attitude to adopt. The heirs of Pyrrhonic scepticism were the philosophers of the New Academy whose opinions were elegantly represented for Augustine by the writings of Cicero. To find a positive basis for knowledge was for the young Augustine a task not of playful dialectics but of anxious moral concern. For he could advance no step towards the beliefs which his soul desired without establishing confidence in know-ledge.

[1] De lib. arb. II. v. 11; P.L. xxxii. 1245.
[2] *Introduction à l'étude de St. Augustin*, Paris, 1929, p. 294.

It was, as we have seen, the study of the Platonists which led him
to a positive basis for knowledge; but the discovery is expressed in
a form peculiarly his own. The argument is given in a number of
passages throughout his works.[1] The substance of these passages is
twofold. Firstly, it is argued that the process of doubting presumes
the certain knowledge that something exists, namely the doubter
and his mental activities. Secondly, the criticism of knowledge
implies a criterion of truth.

The principles of nature are obscure. Men have disputed, for
example, whether the energy of life is derived from air or from fire,
whether the self is simple or complex. Philosophers have even
impugned the evidence of our senses. Yet there is at least one fact
which no one, however sceptical, càn call in question, namely the
existence of himself. Though I doubt, I am aware of myself as
existing when I doubt. *Si fallor sum.* Even if I suppose my
experience to be an illusion or a dream I must assume that I exist.
And this conviction provides a ground for knowledge. Using less
ambiguous terms than Descartes, whose famous argument these
passages so fully anticipates,[2] Augustine maintains that the primary intuition of the self includes all the processes which can be
abstractly distinguished within it. It includes desiring, remember-
ing, willing, thinking, feeling. More summarily, it comprises a
direct apprehension, a judgement, and a feeling. 'I am most
certain that I am, and that I know this and enjoy it.'

This truth is immediately perceived. Whatever doubts philosophers have thrown on the reports of the senses concerning the
external world, they have never been able to disprove truths of
this character.[3] For (as we shall discover) Augustine thinks there
are other truths of the same order.

Now the crucial question for Augustine, as for Descartes, is
what is further implied by this intuition of the self as to the fundamental nature of knowledge. We are left in no doubt. In the
passage in *De civitate Dei* it is said: 'We do not discern these ideas
through some bodily sense as we apprehend colours, sounds, and
tastes; but without any delusive representation (*ludificatoria
imaginatione*) of spurious perception or of images (*phantasiarum
vel phantasmatum*) I am most certain that I am and that I know
this and enjoy it.' Elsewhere the mind is said to know this truth

---

[1] Cf. Solil. ii. 1, P.L. xxxii. 885; De Trin. x. x. 14, P.L. xlii. 981; De civ. Dei·
xi. 26, C.S.E.L. xL. i. 551.

[2] Cf. Meditations, ii.   [3] De Trin. xv. xii. 21; P.L. xlii. 1073.

'of itself'. It knows itself through itself, because it is incorporeal.[1]
It perceives itself 'not by a movement through space, but by an
incorporeal reversion to itself'.[2]   This knowledge, in a word, is
detached from all contact with the data of sense-perception.   The
mind knows the external world indirectly.   Awareness of the self
as continuous and permanent—and the self without these characteristics vanishes from view—is derived not from the continuity
and coherence of the objective world, but from a disembodied
entity.   In fact, as we shall see, Augustine believes that the mind
produces its experience from its own resources.

Thus the ground of certitude points to a radical dualism in
knowledge ; and perceptual experience occupies from the outset a
secondary position.

In the second line of attack upon scepticism which is found in
Augustine's writings he is standing on firmer ground.   He argues
that scepticism assumes a criterion of truth.   To be conscious
that I am deceived presumes some awareness of what constitutes
reality.   And the cardinal principle which is thus revealed is the
principle of non-contradiction or, in positive terms, of coherence.
We may not know what quality a thing in reality possesses.   But
we know that it cannot both have a particular quality and not
have it.   The same mind cannot both perish and be immortal ; if
the world contains only four elements it cannot contain five.[3]
This principle gives a positive guide to knowledge, a clue to its
general nature.   But again the question arises whether it gives any
but a formal content to knowing apart from reference to sense-
experience.

We meet at this point with a distinctive feature of Augustine's
discussions on truth.   He is 'the master of the inner life'.   His
powers of psychological introspection were exceptional, and his
pages contain many valuable observations of mental processes.[4]
But more than this, he is always bidding us look within ourselves
to find the gateway to virtue and to knowledge.   The moral law is
written in our hearts ; and the first step to truth is to be thoroughly
acquainted with oneself.   'Go not outside thyself, but return within
thyself ; for truth resides in the inmost part of man.'[5]   This subjective note, first and chiefly struck by Augustine, divides ancient

[1] De Trin. IX. iii. 3 ; P.L. xlii. 963.
[2] De Trin. XIV. vi. 8 ; P.L. xlii. 1042.
[3] Contra Acad. III. xiii. 29 ; C.S.E.L. lxiii. 68.
[4] See J. Morgan, *The Psychological Teaching of St. Augustine*, London, 1932.
[5] De vera rel. xxix. 72 ; P.L. xxxii. 154.

philosophy from medieval and modern speculation. Christianity
and the decay of civilization had transferred the direction of
intellectual endeavour from the outer world to the soul. The forms
of relation characteristic of mental life were raised to the status of
metaphysical principles; and the processes of will, of memory,
and of thought were applied to the operations of reality.

But the truth reached by the inner path is anything but subjective. If our ideas did not refer to an independent and objective
realm, no discussion would be possible between men. Everyone
would be confined to their own ideas, and *quot homines tot senten-
tiae*.[1] The region of reality is the world of Ideas, necessary, immutable, intelligible.

Augustine's main concern is this realm of Ideas, and he constantly seeks to show that they are integral to thought, even at the
lowest levels. Fundamentally knowledge is one. But it expresses
itself in two ways, which are distinguished as lower and higher
reason. The former is further termed *Scientia*. *Scientia* is defined
as the knowledge of temporal and changing things necessary for
prosecuting the activities of this life.[2] Its spring is practical.
The higher reason is *Sapientia*, wisdom. Its motive is contemplation and its objects the intelligible Ideas. Thus action is subordinate to contemplation.

Let us now trace the steps by which Augustine advances from
bare sensation to the knowledge of *intelligibiles res*.

IV

The interesting point about Augustine's account of perception
is the way in which the isolation of the mind from its objects is
preserved. This separation foreshadows the representative or indirect theory of perception, which in a scientific setting formed the
basis of theories of knowledge in the seventeenth and eighteenth
centuries.

The theory is determined by the nature of the mind and its
relation to the body. The mind is wholly different in substance
from the body. It is, in comparison with the body, simple, while
being present as a whole everywhere throughout the body.[3] The

---

[1] De lib. arb. II. x. 28; P.L. xxxii. 1256.

[2] De Trin. XII. xii. 17; P.L. xlii. 1007. The chief value conceded to *Scientia* is
that it provides an opportunity by which the Faith may be supported and
defended. Cf. De Trin. XIV. i. 3; P.L. xlii. 1037.

[3] De Trin. VI. vi. 8; P.L. xlii. 929. Strictly speaking, *anima*, which is used
throughout this discussion, means the vital animating function of *animus*, the
substantial mind. *Animus* contains thought (*mens*) as well as life (*anima*).

body is regarded as belonging entirely to the physical order. Its parts change and decay, but (save for a certain spontaneity attributed to light) it is subject only to external influences. The principle upon which Augustine insists in contrasting the two substances is that mind is always active, body always passive. The notion underlying this contrast has nothing to do with the Cartesian dualism of mechanical extended substance and unextended thinking substance, though the outcome is similar. The principle is rooted in the Neoplatonic and theological view of the mind as a symbol and vehicle of the spiritual order; and it carries with it the consequences frequently dwelt on by Augustine. 'The idea that the body can make any impression on the spirit cannot be seriously maintained, as though the spirit were subject to the motions of the body in the same way as matter. For what acts is in every way more excellent than that which it acts on.'[1] The mind, ever active, animates a body ever passive; and the body has no influence on the mind's activity. How, then, are the processes of sensation and perception to be explained? The influences which play upon the body cannot be transmitted by way of the sense-organs to consciousness; for the sense-organs are as physical as any other portions of matter, and can only affect matter. Motions striking upon the ear, for example, do not produce impressions on the mind. 'When we hear, the rhythms which occur in the mind are not produced by those rhythms which we know to be in the sounds themselves.' We may postpone for the moment the problem how the rhythms in the sounds themselves are known. Let us first inquire how the sensory qualities are perceived.

Augustine's explanation, to which medieval theories of perception frequently recur, is given most clearly in the passage in *De musica* that follows the quotation which has been given above. Some extracts from this passage may be given:

'For my part I hold that the body is only animated by the mind in a directive manner (*intentione facientis*). . . . Any physical objects which penetrate or press on the body from outside, affect not the mind but the body only, so as to hinder or promote its functions. Accordingly, when it struggles against resistance, and experiences difficulty in controlling the material forces thrust against it, a heightened awareness results (*fit attentior*) owing to the difficulty of acting, and this attention to difficulty, when it reaches the level of consciousness, is sensation, and is

---

[1] De Gen. ad litt. xii. 16; C.S.E.L. xxviii. 1, 402: cf. De Musica, VI. v; P.L. xxxii. 1167. St. Augustine understands by *musica* not the art of singing or playing but the science of the laws which regulate harmony and rhythm.

described as pain or effort. . . . In a word it seems to me that the mind when it experiences sensation in the body receives no impression from it, but becomes more attentive to impressions on the body. These acts of attention appear to the mind as pleasant when the body's functions are promoted, disagreeable when they are frustrated. The total effect is what is known as sensation. But the apprehension which, even when we are aware of no sensation, is present in us, is the body's organ, and this is controlled by the mind, so that it becomes better prepared to deal with effects in the body, admitting what is appropriate and rejecting what is harmful. . . . Now when those influences occur which produce, so to speak, differences in the body, the mind exerts efforts of attention appropriate to each of its parts and organs, and is said to see, to hear, to smell, to taste, or to sense by touch. . . . These are the activities by which, in my view, the mind meets the impressions of the body when it experiences sensation. I do not believe it directly receives the impressions.'[1]

To grasp St. Augustine's meaning we must explore a little further the implications of the *intentione facientis*. For him the fundamental characteristic of mind is not cognitive but conative. A form of will precedes the expression of sensation. 'Prius enim quam visio fieret jam voluntas.' This fundamental teleological activity of the mind has a vegetative and an animal level which are described at length in *De quantitate animae*.[2] Its functions at these levels are to preserve the body's organic unity, to nourish it, to cause its growth and reproduction, to direct its movements and its perceptions. Sensation is thus related, as we should say, to biological function. Normally this level of mind acts without consciousness. It informs and directs the sense-organs. 'Vitali motu in silentio corpus aurium vegetebat.' The mind secretly sustains by its living activity the organ of hearing. When, owing to obstruction, there is enhancement of effort the sensation becomes conscious. But—and this is the essential feature of the theory—the independence of the two orders is strictly retained. The mind watches over and manages the body, observing the impressions which fall upon it. Some it ignores; a mass of them it reproduces from its own nature and informs with these elementary and barely conscious reproductions, the body's sense-organs; some it recreates as emotions and desires. The images or impressions of bodies are

---

[1] De mus. VI. v. 9, 10; P.L. xxxii. 1168-9. This passage should be compared with the account of vision in *De Trin.* XI. ii. 2-5, where the role of sense is described in more passive terms. But even here it is said that 'for him who sees there is the sense of sight and the intention of looking at and attending to the object'.

[2] Op. cit. xxxiii. 71; P.L. xxxii. 1074.

fashioned by the mind 'of its own substance'.[1] 'It is not the body that feels but the mind through the body, which it uses as a messenger. in order to produce within itself what is announced outside.'[2] The mind can form images without the intervention of the body.

The theory is striking. It recognizes in a remarkable way the conative origin of consciousness to which modern psychology has returned. Primitive awareness is traced to tensions set up by physical obstructions. But the parallelism of body and mind is preserved at some cost. It is difficult to grasp what 'being attentive to' and 'watching over' the body can mean unless the physical accompaniment of such processes is illogically assumed. It will be noticed, too, that in spite of the initial distinction between the nature of mind and body, an independent activity is allowed to the body. Further, from the point of view of the theory of knowledge we may ask how far sensations, if they are made by the mind, represent reality.

It is doubtful whether this question would have troubled Augustine. Sometimes he leaps the difficulty by asserting that the object and the similitude of it wrought in sensation are alike.[3] At other times he assumes that the 'senses' of the mind reproduce the 'form', that is to say, the actual nature of the object. But his essential reply is that the question of objectivity does not arise in relation to *sensibilia*. The apprehensions of the senses are not themselves true or false. If we ask whether the object is as it appears to be, whether the oar which appears broken in the water is in fact broken, we appeal not to the senses but to the judgement. It is precisely because the sceptics confine themselves to the witness of the senses that knowledge becomes impossible for them.[4]

The sensory elements are not the primary entities of knowledge. In *De libero arbitrio*[5] it is pointed out that in addition to the reports of the separate senses which give us colour, sound, flavour, smoothness, and so forth, there are other qualities pertaining to the form of bodies, the qualities of being large, small, square, and round, which we do not perceive by any one sense. These non-sensory perceptions are referred in the Aristotelian manner to 'a certain inner sense to which all things are reported from the familiar five

[1] De Trin. x. v. 7; P.L. xlii. 977.
[2] De Gen. ad litt. xii. 24; C.S.E.L. xxviii. 1, 416.
[3] De Trin. xi. iii. 6; P.L. xlii. 989.
[4] Contra Acad. iii. xi. 26; C.S.E.L. lxiii. 67.
[5] De lib. arb. ii. vii, viii; P.L. xxxii. 1249–53.

senses'. And this common interior sense is present in the minds of
animals; in virtue of it they avoid what is displeasing and pursue
what is pleasing to them. In modern terms its province is the
instinctive life.

In an interesting discussion in *De quantitate animae*[1] various
elements of perception which are not derived from sensation are
traced. These elements are said to be 'presumed or inferred'.
The discussion is in the form of a dialogue. Perception is first
defined as bare apprehension by the mind of what affects the body.
'Sensum puto esse non latere animam quod patitur corpus.' But,
it is pointed out, if this *non latere animam* means an isolated
and immediate mental element, difficulties arise. In the first place,
vision does not consist only of an immediate image in the sense-
organ. Unless it were to include more than this we should see no
more than our own eyes. Distance or spatial reference is implied in
the act of seeing. In the second place we perceive more than that
which sight alone gives, even when it is thus complicated. For
example, we perceive fire, though our actual image is that of smoke.
Already we are beginning to be aware that perception is a kind of
knowledge through sensation. In addition to the image, which
reproduces the impression on the organs of the body, something else
is presumed or inferred. A further example of what is not known
by sensation, taken literally, is the fact of growth. 'It is one thing
to see nails longer, another to know that they grow.' Considerations such as these compel us to revise our definition. There is a
sensum, we must say, which is an impression on the body of which
the mind is barely (*per se*) aware without the intervention of any
other factor. Every impression on the body of which the mind is
barely aware is this *sensum*, but every *sensum* is not simply this.
It may be complicated by perspective and by meaning, in the sense
suggested above. Lastly, the current division between the minds
of animals and of men is adduced. Surely, it is suggested, Odysseus'
dog, which recognized him after twenty years, displayed more than
'bare perception'. Its recognition of its master is obviously more
than this. What it lacked, however, was the human characteristic
of knowing that it recognized its master. We must, in fact,
distinguish two types of perception, perception *per rationem* and
perception *per corpus*. But even the latter, which is common to
men and animals, includes more than bare apprehension. And
human perception points beyond, to *scientia*.

[1] Op. cit. xxiii–xxvi; P.L. xxxii. 1058–65.

To these considerations we may add passages in which retention as a factor in perception is discussed. It is observed, for example, that in hearing the briefest syllable, *a fortiori* a word of several syllables, unless the motion of the beginning of the syllable were retained in our mind when the ending is uttered, we should not hear it at all, still less understand it. Perceiving is more than sensing.

These suggestions are neither clearly nor fully worked out. They serve to indicate the mental and formal characteristics of elementary knowledge; and these characteristics lead Augustine quickly to the further stages of his ascent towards reality. But the next phase in the development of knowledge is still more summarily treated. For at this point the development of general ideas—man, colour, triangularity—naturally falls to be described. But the recognition of common qualities which enable us to think of objects and to predicate their qualities does not arise for Augustine through the process of generalizing the particular given elements. No account of the formation of concept by comparison and abstraction can be found in his writings. He speaks frequently of the way in which the images of things perceived by the senses are retained in the memory. Sensation reproduces the species of the corporeal thing; these images are formed in the memory, and the *visio cogitantis* is fashioned from the memory images.[1] But abstraction in the Aristotelian sense, by which general concepts are derived from sensory impressions, is foreign to his outlook. For the Aristotelian account is founded on the belief that the body and the physical world act upon the mind; and we have seen that Augustine does not admit this.

On the one hand, sensation is necessary for a knowledge of things. On the other hand, sensory perception implies, as we have seen, general notions 'inferred or assumed'. But beyond this it must be admitted that it is difficult to discover any further psychological account. We have pointed out above that psychological analysis is, for Augustine, incidental to the problem of truth. It is from this point of view that we must interpret his references to general ideas.

He is interested, not in the formation of concepts, but in the criteria of truth contained in them. To speak, for example, of the human mind *specialiter et generaliter*, that is of the generic human mind, is to refer to the truth. 'We do not gather a notion of the

[1] De Trin. xi. ix; P.L. xlii. 996. Cf. iii. 6 of the same book.

human mind in its general character by comparison, observing a number of minds with bodily eyes; we contemplate indestructible truth, by means of which we define precisely, as far as we can, not the nature of one particular man's mind, but the nature it ought to be according to the eternal reasons.'[1] It is assumed that general notions are entirely independent of sensible origin, in the same way as the notions of truth, coherence, equality, and number. Their content comes 'from above'. The mind refers the intelligible norms which it contemplates above it to the sensations and images derived from its commerce with the body and with physical objects. *Scientia* is rooted in perception, but it is not derived from the flux of sensations. And since *scientia*, the farther it advances, is increasingly concerned with the 'reasons', numbers, and forms of things, it does not require the process of abstraction from particular sensations. For these Ideas are discussed without reference to the sensible world. 'But that capacity of ours which is concerned with the treatment of corporeal and temporal things is, indeed, rational in that it is not common to us and the beasts, but is drawn, as it were, out of that rational substance of our mind by which we are in contact with the intelligible and immutable truth, and which is deputed to handle and direct the inferior things.'[2]

Thus the perception of the world depends on the activity of intellectual apprehension, and this in turn upon the eternal reasons. The analysis of knowledge is dominated everywhere by the Platonic Ideas. We are drawn quickly in all Augustine's discussions on knowledge to the sphere of timeless entities.

V

But before we enter on those conceptions which occupy the central interest of Augustine's thought we may glance at his general attitude to the 'rational knowledge of temporal things'. Many writers have made play with utterances in which he appears to deprecate scientific inquiry into the operations of nature. Some of these frequently quoted remarks demand to be read in their context. Thus the passage in the *Confessions*[3] about 'vain and curious desire, veiled under the name of knowledge' refers to magical and superstitious inquiries. And the saying in *The City of*

[1] De Trin. ix. vi. 9; P.L. xlii. 966, 955.
[2] De Trin. xii. iii. 3; P.L. xlii. 999.
[3] x. xxv. 54, 55.

God,[1] that the knowledge of temporal things with which devils are puffed up is contemptible to angels, must be connected with the preceding passage in which the defect in the knowledge possessed by devils is pointed out. What is wrong with devils' knowledge is not that it is concerned with temporal things, but that it lacks charity. Texts can indeed be cited in which empirical knowledge is slightingly spoken of;[2] but this is a different matter to disparaging a scientific understanding of Nature. For Augustine's view of natural knowledge was Platonic, and the empirical method was deemed subordinate to the mathematical. He emphatically warns Christians against the danger of clinging to crude beliefs about the natural world on the authority of Scripture.

'It frequently happens that there is some question about the earth, or the sky, or the other elements of this world, the movement, revolutions, or even the size and distance of the stars, the regular eclipses of the sun and the moon, the course of the years and seasons; the nature of the animals, vegetables, and minerals, and other things of the same kind, respecting which one who is not a Christian has knowledge derived from most certain reasoning or observation. And it is highly deplorable and mischievous and a thing especially to be guarded against that he should hear a Christian speaking of such matters in accordance with Christian writings and uttering such nonsense that, knowing him to be as wide of the mark as, to use the common expression, east is from west, the unbeliever can scarcely restrain himself from laughing.'[3]

In his allusions to the scientific theories of his age Augustine shows caution. He confesses that he has not been able to spare the time to grasp the subtle and difficult questions of cosmology.[4] But he expresses admiration of the work of the astronomers, contrasting their mathematical calculations of the solstices, equinoxes, and eclipses with the fables of the Manichees.[5] He adheres to the doctrine of the four elements, in which earth as the heaviest element is always seeking the lowest place, while water, air, and fire are ranged above in ascending order.[6] He devotes much attention to the theory of primary matter. The problem arises in connexion with the interpretation of the phrases of Genesis, such as the phrase 'the earth was without form'. Augustine conceives a formless substance endowed with a lowly life, which underlies the definite forms of things. It is the substratum of change.[7]

[1] Op. cit. IX. xxii; C.S.E.L. xl. i. 439.
[2] Cf. De an. IV. x. 14; P.L. xliv. 532, and Encheiridion, ix.
[3] De Gen. ad litt. I. xix; C.S.E.L. xxviii. i. 28.
[4] Ib. II. x; C.S.E.L. xxviii. i. 48.   [5] Confess. v. iii. 6.
[6] De civ. Dei. XXII. xi; C.S.E.L. xl. ii. 616.   [7] Confess. XII. vi 6

It has been pointed out that all Augustine's discussions of physics refer to Platonic theories, not to Aristotelian.[1] This preference was felt till the twelfth century. The principal pagan authors studied on points of cosmology were Chalcidius, Martianus Capella, and Macrobius; and their Platonic theories accorded with the teaching of Augustine, whose writings were the chief Christian authority for physical beliefs. Thus, through him, the *Timaeus* determined the scientific framework of the succeeding centuries.

One side of Augustine's teaching on nature has stirred peculiar interest in modern times. This is his discussion of the creation of biological species. Many commentators have detected a theory of evolution in the account of 'seminal reasons' given in *De Genesi ad litteram*. The question arises for him not from any direct interest in the biological relation of species to one another, but from difficulties in the story of creation given in the early chapters of Genesis. The text clearly signifies that God created all things at one instant; for, argues Augustine, the six days of creation cannot be taken in their literal sense. But in the second chapter of Genesis the appearance of creatures, including man, plainly takes place in a temporal succession. Further, countless new individual creatures have appeared since the first creation of species. The problem is to reconcile these two principles found in Scripture, the total creation of the world and its inhabitants at one moment, and the successive appearance of species and of individuals. The problem has nothing to do with the modification of species by descent.

Augustine meets the apparent contradiction by supposing that the act of creation took place in two stages. In the first stage plants, animals, and men are created potentially and simultaneously, in the second they actually and successively appear. In the first stage creatures are said to be made in their 'seminal reasons'. *Rationes seminales* are interpreted in a variety of ways. They are said to be the germs of seeds of living beings. In other passages they are described as existing in an indeterminate fluid state which precedes the emergence of the seed, and which is invisible to the human eye. This state, in some passages, is still more abstractly defined as a generative power, and even as a law of growth. On the whole it is manifest that the seminal reasons are intended to be activities which determine the fact and order of growth. These forces imply no doctrine of preformism—the germ does not contain the subsequent individual in a contracted form. 'Let us consider the beauty

---

[1] Cf. P. Duhem, *Système du Monde*, Paris, 1913–17, ii, 410.

of some tree, with its trunk, branches, leaves, and fruit. We not only know that this appearance and size have not suddenly come about, but we know also in what order. For the tree began with the root which the germ first fixed in the ground, and from thence all this developed form has grown. Moreover, that germ came from a seed; therefore all these features were in the seed originally, not in a mass of corporeal magnitude, but in a force and causal potency.'[1] But this potential state signifies a predestined development. 'If the causes of all future things were placed in the world when God created all things together, . . . those causes contained not only that man could be made thus, but truly also that he had to be made thus.'[2] But God may modify their effects. Augustine draws a significant conclusion, that it is vain to seek causes for all phenomena.[3] The essential point is that the seminal reasons are conceived within the framework of fixed species. Nowhere does Augustine envisage a development from one species to a different species. It is true that the parent of trees and of animals is said to be the earth.[4] But the active causality which is contained in the earth is specified to produce its kind. God created, at the beginning, seminal reasons appropriate to all species. 'But as in that grain of seed there are together invisibly all those things which develop into a tree in the course of time, so we must think of the world as having together, when God created all things at once, all those things which were in it and with it when the day was made' . . . including 'all those things which the waters and the earth produced potentially and causally before they were to arise in the course of time as they are now known to us.'[5]

The doctrine that all creatures which will appear to the end of time were created *potentialiter et causaliter* has an important corollary. The voluntary activity of created beings cannot produce any genuinely new being. All it can do in this direction is to provide the external conditions for such production. The creation of substantial existence is only possible to God, working through the seminal reasons.

In his book on St. Augustine,[6] Mr. Hugh Pope has collected a large number of examples of his 'devouring curiosity' over natural

---

[1] De Gen. ad litt. v. 23; C.S.E.L. xxviii. i. 167. The translations given here are those of Dr. E. C. Messenger, to whose discussion of the seminal reasons in *Evolution and Theology*, London, 1931, I am greatly indebted.
[2] Op. cit. vi. 18; C.S.E.L. xxviii. i. 192.   [3] Ib. vi. 16; C.S.E.L. xxviii. i. 191.
[4] Ib. v. 23; C.S.E.L. xxviii. i. 168.   [5] Ib.
[6] *Saint Augustine of Hippo*, London, 1937, chapter vi.

phenomena, especially in the provinces of physiology and of animal behaviour. Augustine even conducted some experiments; he tested, for instance, the belief that the flesh of the peacock does not putrefy. But when all is said, his scientific knowledge, even for the age, is meagre. And it is manifest that the investigation of natural processes for their own sake is fundamentally opposed to his general attitude to knowledge. He frequently warns Christians against vain curiosity which turns the mind away from the contemplation of eternal things.[1] Science must be strictly subordinated to philosophy, that is to say, to the pursuit of wisdom.[2]

This conception of the value of science was prevalent in the age of decadence. The Roman moralists no less than the Neoplatonic philosophers regarded independent inquiry into natural causes as an inferior and elementary activity of mind.[3] The religious mind of the age contributed to this attitude. It accepted the phenomena of nature as the manifestations of God. For precise scrutiny it substituted allegorical interpretation. And for Augustine this method of approach to Nature is supported by his theory of knowledge. He was deeply interested, throughout his life, in the nature of learning. He discusses its psychology at length in *De magistro*.[4] He shows that words, written or uttered, and indeed any significant symbol, are merely the stimuli for capacities which exist already in the mind. The arguments of the teacher are invitations to the learner to 'return to himself', and to discover within the truths that dwell there. Not that these truths are innate, in the sense that men are endowed with them at birth. Still less are they the memories of previous existence, as in the Platonic doctrine of reminiscence. They exist, as we have seen, in the ideal realm which the mind is formed to enter if it will. Now if we try to explain the way in which the human mind acquires its knowledge we find a close parallel between the apprehension of ideas and the apprehension of sensations. We have seen that the mind uses the body 'as a kind of messenger in order to reproduce from within itself what is announced outside'. The messages which the forms and movements of the world bring are spiritual truths.[5] They are patterns or symbols of the moral reality which sustains phenomena. The causal connexions of nature do not embody a structure

---

[1] Cf. De mus. VI. xiii. 39; P.L. xxxii. 1184.
[2] Cf. De Ord. I. viii. 24; C.S.E.L. lxiii. 137.
[3] Cf. for example Seneca, Ep. 88.
[4] Op. cit. Cap. ii ff.; P.L. xxxii. 1196.
[5] Cf. Gilson, *Introduction à l'étude de S. Augustin*, p. 93.

independent of, and indifferent to, man's desires. They are to be viewed teleologically, as means for the instruction of the soul.

This conception hastened the eclipse of scientific investigation. St. Augustine's writings are filled with fanciful analogies between natural phenomena and theological truths. The moon is a symbol of the Church which reflects the divine light; the wind is an image of the spirit; numbers are significant of moral or theological ideas; the number eleven, for instance, stands for sin, for eleven 'transgresses' ten, and ten signifies the law, because of its association with the commandments. The psychological analogies in *De Trinitate* are on a different plane.

In a word, little importance attached to nature in itself. The earth and the stars, trees and animals, convey obscure messages of God's purpose to the human mind.

VI

The mind possesses the power through its bodily senses of perceiving physical objects; it has also the power of discerning the self, and things which though resembling bodies are not corporeal; and lastly it can contemplate objects which are neither bodies nor like bodies; things which have neither colour nor passion, nor any such quality. And it is on such things we ought most intently to dwell.[1] Again 'the intellectual cognition of eternal things is one thing, the rational cognition of temporal things is another; and no one doubts that the former is to be preferred to the latter'.[2] The entire trend of Augustine's analysis of knowledge is towards the establishment of a region of immutable certainty. The relativity of sensory perception requires the regulative power of thought or judgement. It is the fact that the mind appreciates a rule or principle which is important. The mind corrects the impressions of the senses, such as the bent appearance of an oar in water,[3] by reference to a reality, the physical object, which is known by thought. But the mind is compelled to advance beyond this stage. For the judgement of truth and reality is here fallible. In so far as it bears upon the changing scene of events, it is infected with the relativity of their being. Constantly the mind in judging of the truth of appearances, appeals to principles which are untouched by the shifting tide of visible things. The exploration of these principles

---

[1] De an. IV. xx. 31; P.L. xliv. 542.
[2] De Trin. XII. xv. 25; P.L. xlii. 1012.   [3] Cf. p. 15 above.

discovers an intelligible structure in the world. And this structure is timeless.

The approach, then, to these realities lies through the recognition by the judgement of necessary criteria. Now what principles are there of this nature? There are according to Augustine many types of such principles. An important class is the class of mathematical ideas, or more generally, principles of order, rhythm, and symmetry. Mathematical ideas are types of being which are not subject to change; they are certain; and they are not dependent upon the nature of the mind which approaches them.

'The reason and truth of number is present to all who reflect, so that everyone who calculates tries to apprehend it with his reason and understanding. It offers itself equally to all who can grasp it; nor when perceived by anyone is it changed and altered for the nutriment, as it were, of its perceiver; nor does it cease when someone is deceived in it, but he is so much the more in error the less he sees it, while it remains true and whole.'[1]

Seven and three, Augustine adds, are ten, not only now but always.

The vital question for Augustine's theory of knowledge concerns the relation of such Ideas to sensible objects. It is indeed the vital question for medieval philosophy. In treating of mathematical Ideas the question is candidly faced. 'Supposing', he asks, 'someone were to say to you that these numbers are not apprehended by our mind through some property peculiar to them, but that we receive impressions of them in the same way as certain images of things seen which are derived from corporeal objects, how would you answer?' Evodius is made to reply that even if numbers are derived from the senses, the judgements of arithmetic, by which we can detect errors in addition or subtraction, are not so derived. We perceive the truth that seven and three are ten 'by the light of the mind'. And this is a truth which has a permanence that no physical object possesses. It does not, therefore, depend on sensible objects. Further, any sensible object is capable of infinite division. No body, however small, is a simple unity. But to know that no body is one is to know what one is. And this knowledge is not drawn from acquaintance with bodies, that is to say from sense-perception. Lastly, it is pointed out that in mathematical calculations it is possible to transcend the bounds of space and time and predict results throughout infinity. Take any simple arithmetical process, such as the multiplication of a number by two,

[1] De lib. arb. II. viii. 20; P.L. xxxii. 1251.

and a rule becomes evident to the mind, which applies to all possible numbers. How can this truth be contemplated so surely through countless numbers save by an inner light which the bodily senses do not know?[1]

From these considerations it is concluded that mathematical ideas are one class of realities—and 'there are many such things'[2] —which are in no way inventions of the mind, which are free of the flux of space and time, and which evince a logical system of relations which are necessary and do not, in consequence, depend upon any accumulation of instances. And being themselves non-sensory they are discovered by a process of mind which is independent of sense-perception.

These arguments point to a realm of reality which appears to be completely sundered from the world as it is perceived to exist. Not only do the two regions, the region of Ideas and the region of perception, have no connexion with one another, but the manner by which each is apprehended, the way of sensory-perception and the way of thought tend also to fall apart. Augustine's arguments forcibly suggest the presence in experience of a fundamental structure which is non-sensory, which *intellectus* apprehends. But so far as these arguments go, the operations adduced do not warrant the conclusion that there are two worlds and two ways of knowing them. The truths of arithmetic are not independent of empirical experience. In adding or multiplying we direct attention solely to the quantitative aspect of things. But an aspect is not an independent order. Mathematical propositions concern, not a radically distinct region of experience, but certain formal charac-teristics of the perceived world. And taken apart from that world they give but abstract knowledge. The knowledge what one is is not knowledge of reality until we know what things are one.

But such criticisms are only applicable at this stage of Augustine's description of Ideas. The abrupt severance of the worlds of sense and of thought must be considered from another angle. The Ideas are not merely intelligible systems standing contrasted with the irrational flux of corporeal objects. Knowledge of Ideas is funda-mental for the knowledge of corporeal things. Number lies at the basis of reality. Mathematical Ideas are generalized, and appear under the forms of order, rhythm, symmetry, harmony. From these

[1] Ib. II. viii. 23; P.L. xxxii. 1253.
[2] Ib. II. viii. 20; P.L. xxxii. 1251.   In *De Trin.* IX. vi. 9–11 norms of truth, beauty, and goodness are named.

principles the objects of perception derive their existence. 'They do not come into being nor perish, but it is through them that all things which can or do come into being or perish are made.'[1] 'Look upon the sky and the earth and the sea and all the things which shine in them or above them, or creep or fly or swim beneath them. They have forms because they have numbers; take that from them and they will cease to be.'[2] Thus the object of our perception as well as those of our scientific understanding derive their substantial being from mathematical forms. In so far as our intellect discerns the rhythmic order in corporeal things, it discerns reality. These forms are the prototypes of the objects presented to our senses. Things exist primarily in their eternal Ideas, but they exist also for us in their material mode.[3] And they exist in the Ideas not only as species or genera but also as individuals.[4] For the doctrine is put forward in close connexion with the interpretation of the work of creation described in Genesis.

We are now in a better position to appreciate the grounds upon which Augustine believes in the external order of objects perceived. The mind, we have seen, has no direct awareness of bodies through the sense; it forms images of them from within itself. Nevertheless 'objects exist without being perceived, and sound exists when there are no ears to hear'.[5] The existence of material bodies in the physical guise in which they appear to us, or, more strictly, in the manner in which the mind reproduces them, remains a point not of knowledge but of belief. This belief is a necessary postulate of practical life. But through 'the mist of corporeal images' the intellect descries the immutable Forms which constitute the stable reality of things. The sensible image is for our feeble minds a necessary aid to the intellectual apprehension of the unchanging Form. For man's thought does not dwell, for example, on the incorporeal and immutable form of a square body in the same way as that form itself remains in it; if indeed the mind could have arrived at the form apart from the image of enclosed space.[6] The mind is helped to intellectual understanding of the eternal structure of the world by 'the transient glance' of sensory perception. But 'if you have looked upon anything mutable, you cannot grasp

[1] De div. quaest. qu. 46; P.L. xl. 30.
[2] De lib. arb. II. 42; P.L. xxxii. 1263.
[3] De vera rel. xxii. 42. P.L. xxxiv. 40.
[4] Epist. xiv. 4; P.L. xxxiii. 80.
[5] De mus. VI. ii. 3; P.L. xxxii. 1164.
[6] De Trin. XII. xiv. 23; P.L. xlii. 1011; cf. ib. XI. l. 1; P.L. xlii. 984.

it by the sense of the body or by the consideration of the mind, unless it is held firmly by some form of numbers; and if they are removed it falls back again into nothing'.[1] The mind is led to a knowledge of numbers through the sensible quality of objects, but apart from numbers there would be no object to perceive.

This fundamental order is at the opposite pole of being to mechanism. Augustine frequently associates with quantitative terms such as number or magnitude, terms expressing aesthetic natures. In a remarkable passage in the section of *De libero arbitrio* from which we have been quoting it is asserted that art is number. 'Human artists too have numbers of all bodily forms in art, and it is to them they shape their works. In fashioning they move their hands and instruments until that which is formed outside is referred back to that light of numbers which is within.' The motion of the artist's arms is number; and if we ask what it is that pleases in a dance 'number will answer you, Behold it is I'.[2] *Numeri* reveal at once the rhythmic beauty and the intelligible necessity of the natural world.

But mathematical Ideas are types of reality to which our judgement in every province ultimately refer. The moral principles of practical life rest on immutable standards in which we descry a supreme good, wherein our hearts are fulfilled. 'The rules and certain lights of virtue are true and immutable and are each or all present in common to be contemplated by those who are able to conceive them.'[3] Insight into these principles is *sapientia*, Wisdom.

Finally the question is pressed whether the several classes of universal realities discerned by *sapientia* are aspects of the same fundamental reality. Augustine has no doubt that, in the end, moral wisdom and number are single and identical. 'The learned and the scholarly, the more remote they are from earthly blemish, the more they look upon both number and wisdom in truth itself and hold both dear.'[4] And he seeks to explain the connexion between them by an analogy. As in fire brightness and heat exist together, heat affecting objects which are near it, brightness diffusing its influence more remotely; so rational minds are warm with the fire of wisdom, while bodies are infused with the radiance of numbers. But it is admitted that the question is difficult. Although it cannot be clear to our humble minds whether number is in wisdom

---

[1] De lib. arb. II. xvi. 44; P.L. xxxii. 1264.
[2] Ib. II. xvi. 42; P.L. xxxii. 1263.
[3] Ib. II. x. 29; P.L. xxxii. 1257.　　　　　[4] Ib. 31.

or derived from wisdom or whether both can be shown to be the names
of one thing, this is certainly clear, that both are immutably real.[1]

In the natural sphere, however, the Forms point to a Supreme
Form.

'Doubt not that, in order that these mutable things may not be
checked in their course, but by measured motions and by distinctive
variety of forms bring time to a close like a poem's ending, there must be
some eternal and immutable Form, which is neither extended nor varied
in time, and through which all mutable things can receive a form and
according to their kind fulfil and accomplish their ordered rhythms in
space and time.'[2]

Thus Augustine reaches the goal to which all his exploration of
the degrees of knowledge tends. The norms of truth by which the
mind judges, whether in the realm of nature or of goodness or of
beauty, point to an absolute region of the spirit. So the intimations
of the religious consciousness are confirmed. The argument is one
which has been echoed throughout Christian thought, wherever
the influence of Augustine has penetrated. It is the argument
of Cudworth in the seventeenth century, no less than that of
St. Bonaventure in the thirteenth.

But the process by which the mind approaches the system of
absolute Form is complicated in St. Augustine by the doctrine of
illumination. His writings are filled with metaphors drawn from
light. And in this he follows his masters in philosophy. He tells in
the *Confessions*[3] how he came to perceive, through reading the
Platonists, that the soul of man is lit by the sun of truth. And in
De civitate Dei he recalls the explanation given by Plotinus of the
great passage in the *Republic* where the Form of the Good is
compared with the Sun, 'that not even the spirit which these philosophers hold to be the soul of the Universe draws its joy from any
other source than we ourselves, namely, that light which is not
itself, but by which it was erected; and its understanding reflects
the glory of that Intelligence'.[4]

But Augustine employs the simile in varied ways, and there are
widely diverse interpretations of his meaning. Broadly speaking
there are two groups of texts. In one the light by which the mind
is illuminated refers to the standards of truth, beauty, and goodness which it contemplates above itself. 'That light by which the
mind is enlightened is distinct from it, in order that it may behold

---

[1] De lib. arb. II. x.   [2] Ib. xvi. 44.   [3] VII. xi. 13.
[4] De civ. Dei. x. 2; C.S.E.L. xl. i. 448.

clearly all truths whether in itself or in it.'¹ The doctrine resembles
Descartes's intuition of the 'simple natures'. Here illumination
expresses the goal of intellectual endeavour. Other passages, however, teach that illumination is an active intervention by the
divine power on the mind. The intellect is irradiated by God; it
cannot attain to understanding by its own resources. Here the
mind is given a passive role. The notions of goodness and truth are
impressed on our mind as a seal imprints its shape on wax.² There
appears to be no fundamental opposition between these two
conceptions, and taken together they qualify theological difficulties inherent in each. When Augustine says that the light of truth
is God Himself, it must not be supposed that he tells us that in
apprehending the *rationes* of things we are directly aware of the
divine mind. Malebranche claimed the authority of St. Augustine
for holding that in apprehending the Ideas we are apprehending
the mind of God. And from this position he proceeded to assert
that we perceive corporeal objects 'in God'.³ This is certainly not
Augustine's view. 'Nor is our mind itself competent to see them
(corporeal things) in God, in the actual relations in which they
were created, so as to know their number and magnitude and
degree, even if we do not see them through the bodily senses.'⁴
But bodies are perceived by the senses, and it is only through 'the
cloud of corporeal images' that we can contemplate the Ideas. The
mind though rational and intellectual is a created being, and when
it endeavours to behold the light, it trembles in its weakness, and is
unable to attain to it.⁵ Our categories, for example the category of
substance, cannot be applied to God.⁶ The numbers or principles to
which reason points reflect a light which is beyond them. The
metaphors drawn from light seem to teach, on the one hand, that
the principles which guide experience are realities which the mind
is led to accept; on the other, that the meaning of these realities is
not finally to be appreciated by purely intellectual approach. A
theological and religious standpoint bring a more comprehensive
enlightenment; and the Forms are found to be revelations of God.

VII

St. Augustine dedicated his thought, from his nineteenth year,
to the pursuit of *sapientia*, the contemplation of the divine order

¹ De Gen. ad litt. xii. 31; C.S.E.L. xxviii. i. 425. Cf. Confess. vii. xvii. 23.
² De Trin. xiv. xv. 21; P.L. xlii. 1052.   ³ *Recherche de la Vérité*, iii. 6.
⁴ De Gen. ad litt. v. xvi; C.S.E.L. xxviii. i. 159.
⁵ Ib. xii. 31; C.S.E.L. xxviii. i. 425.   ⁶ De Trin. vii. v. 10; P.L. xlii. 942.

implicit in the changing conditions of human experience. His theory of knowledge is a prolonged vindication of the Neoplatonic idealism through which, as we have seen, he found deliverance from the material philosophy of his early years. All his analyses of the modes of knowing have, indeed, a religious end in view. His treatises often open in a scholarly form, on a point of grammar or the definition of a term. Soon logical and metaphysical implications are debated. The philosophic discussion takes on a religious tone; and theology passes into mysticism and prayer.[1]

His philosophy is presented in a series of detached passages, which are often lacking in precision and coherence.[2] The allusiveness of his discussions and the fluidity of his terms permitted schools of varied complexion to claim his authority. But he is the principal channel through which the tradition of Greek thought passed into the reflection of Christian Europe. He taught the ages that followed the logical priority in all human experience, theoretical, moral, aesthetic, religious, of an ideal order which supplements the fragmentariness and impermanence of our temporal understanding. The universe is permeated with the divine ideas. And to them are due the order and measure upon which not only corporeal things, but also the activities of life are based.

In relation to the discussions which follow, the chief point of interest is the sanction thus given to Realism. The general features of experience and thought, the common elements in virtue of which we recognize particular men as men, or dwell in thought upon shape, or justice or knowledge, are entities subsisting beyond the sensible world, though the objects of sense provide information of them. These universal forms constitute the nature of things. They are the true objects of scientific understanding, and the further they are explored the more is revealed of the unchanging origin of the changing world of experience. This is Realism, and we have seen how profoundly it consorts with Christian beliefs. Yet we shall find it, or extreme forms of it, boldly challenged by medieval

---

[1] See, for example, De mus., bk. vi.

[2] The form of the early dialogues, with their long superficial preludes, irrelevant digressions, and verbal disputes, is deliberate. Augustine intended them to be educational exercises for his disciples. As he says, 'the subject could, of course, be concluded in a few words, but I wished to exercise you, and to prove your powers and zeal; for this is my chief concern'. Contra Acad. I. ix. 25. This point is excellently brought out by Marrou, *Saint Augustin et la fin de la culture antique* (Paris, 1938), pp. 298 ff. He shows that the logical disorder of the mature works, such as *De Trinitate*, is also due to a desire to lead the mind, by digressions in many analogous fields, to the contemplation of the objects of pure intelligence.

critics. But the great controversy over universals did not become acute till the appearance of the most formidable of these critics in the eleventh century. The attack of Abaelard upon Realism will be followed in some detail in the next chapter.

The distinctive circle of principles that were first asserted by Augustine persists throughout the course of Western thought; the concentration on the eternal reasons, the doctrine of illumination, the dualism of mind and body, the theory of seminal natures. It is true that from the earliest centuries Aristotelian formulae mingle with this scheme of ideas; they were taught in the Carolingian schools from the text-books of Boethius. But the more fundamental tradition, and that which formed the philosophical structure of Christian belief, was Augustinian. In the eleventh century this implicit tradition became fully articulated in the philosophy of Anselm, who rigorously developed the theological consequences of Realism. Nor did the Augustinian way of thought succumb to the advance of Aristotelianism in the thirteenth century. In fact the metaphysical principles of Aristotle were at first interpreted through the glass of preconceptions that were largely drawn from St. Augustine. When the great Aristotelian-Thomist synthesis of thought appeared, a powerful group of scholars, which included such diverse men as Roger Bacon and St. Bonaventura, asserted the claims of the older view of knowledge in opposition to the new doctrine. And in the following century many distinguished thinkers continued to maintain Augustinian positions in the face of vigorous antagonism. Wyclif, for example, proclaimed an extreme Realism, founded upon the teaching of the Bishop of Hippo. In the period of the Renaissance the philosophy of St. Augustine blended with Platonism, but characteristic features of it appeared in the metaphysics of Descartes. In England, not only arguments from Ideas but also the theory of seminal natures were employed by the Cambridge Platonists in refutation of the new materialism. And the Cambridge Platonists were studied by Coleridge.

These slight references indicate the continuity of the tradition of thought that descended from St. Augustine. But at an early stage of the development of this tradition, in the time of Augustine's greatest disciple, Anselm, there appeared a formidable critic of the orthodox view of knowledge. Abaelard's attack on Realism marks the beginning of a new outlook in philosophy. It prepared the way for the grand reconstructions of the thirteenth century.

II

ABAELARD

REFERENCES

The chief texts used in the following account are the *Logica ingredientibus* and the *Logica nostrorum petitioni sociorum* which are printed in *Beiträge zur Geschichte der Philosophie des Mittelalters*, Band xxi (1919), edited by Dr. Bernhard Geyer, pp. 1–32, and 505–83. A portion of the former work has been translated by R. McKeon in *Selections from Medieval Philosophers*, London, 1930, pp. 208–58.

I

At the opening of the sixth century there appeared at the Court of Theodoric the Goth a scholar whose works exercised a dominant influence upon the thought of the Middle Ages. Boethius was not an original philosopher, but he was a man of eclectic culture, and in an age when few had command even of Latin he was accomplished also in the literature of Greece. His most celebrated work is *The Consolation of Philosophy*, but his philosophical importance depends upon his translations and commentaries. He had studied at Athens and in later years devoted himself to the task of translating and explaining the works of Plato and Aristotle. He succeeded in translating the logical works of Aristotle comprised in the *Organon* before he was put to death on a charge of treason in the year 525. These translations and expositions provided the foundation, until the twelfth century, for the structure of medieval logic.

Among the works of Boethius is a commentary on a treatise composed by Porphyry, a contemporary disciple of Plotinus. Porphyry's treatise is itself an introduction to the *Categories* of Aristotle. In one book of his commentary Boethius, following closely in the steps of his authority, raises a series of questions concerning general ideas or universals. This passage became at a later period the spring from which flowed the copious river of debate concerning Realism and its alternatives. The dispute forms the main theme of our sketch of medieval thought; and it is appropriate at this point to consider broadly the meaning of the issue, and to outline the influences which combined to state it in terms characteristic of medieval philosophy.

In all our perceiving and thinking we find a twofold content. We find throughout our experience singular and general elements in intimate union. The objects we perceive—furniture, people, voices, and guns—are at the same time unique and common to other objects. We perceive *this* book, *that* person; but the book is also *a* book, the person *a* person. Every item to which we direct our attention is an instance of a class or kind. To use medieval terms it is an instance of a species. But the common features in particular objects can be attended to in detachment from the features perceived by the eyes and ears and other senses. To attend to the common elements in abstraction from sensibly perceived objects is to think. We think and speak of books or flowers or bombs in general without referring to any individual book or flower or bomb. And we discuss, and in some cases devote our service to more general entities, shape, colour, learning, beauty, energy, money, the State, Democracy, mysticism. Such entities are universals. The mark of a universal is the presence of elements which appear in a number of things or events numerically distinct. It is an identity in difference. The different elements are the various aspects or instances of an enduring identity which is the subject of our thought and which is fixed in language. And since there is identity in difference throughout the scale of experience, from the perception of a single note of music to the understanding of a philosophical system, universals comprehend the whole range of apprehension and reflection. An inquiry into the nature of universals will embrace the problem of substance, the unity of attributes in things, at one end of the scale; and the validity of the science of physics, or of the Hegelian system, at the other end. It is an inquiry into the veracity of human thinking.

The problem assumed a peculiar importance in the speculation of the Middle Ages for two reasons. It had been transmitted from Greek thought in a manner which distinguished it as the crucial problem for the scientific investigation of the world. And its discussion was profoundly influenced by association with the doctrines of the Christian Faith.

The method of inquiry which is the mark of Scholasticism descends from Socrates and is portrayed in the dialogues of Plato. These conversations discuss the meaning of general notions. They are concerned with asking what some principle really is. Thus the *Charmides* seeks to define the real nature of Temperance, the *Lysis* investigates Friendship, the *Laches*, Courage; and other dialogues examine Love, Virtue, and Justice. In these discussions Socrates criticizes and rejects inadequate definitions with the aim of discovering what essentially characterizes the subject under discussion.

The implications of this method were given far wider significance by Plato. The search for essential characters became the clue to knowledge of reality. The criteria by which we judge what is real in distinction from what is unreal are objectivity, permanence, and coherence. When we reflect on the common-sense world of perception and practical life, we find on all hands variation, indefiniteness, and confusion. The scene which our naïve opinion takes as real is inextricably bound up with our eyes and ears and sense of touch, and varies with changes in them. The hill opposite looks almost perpendicular, the stone feels hot to one hand, lukewarm to the other. Our impressions are corrected by considerations which refer beyond any collection or system of impressions. The further we push the search for consistency and objectivity the more we discover universal relations underlying and connecting the mass of facts with which experience is confronted. The ideal of reason is a system of universals interconnecting all the divisions of reality.

The unities which underlie the changes and the singular aspects of things, beds, or men, or acts of bravery, are not constructions of our minds. They have a being which is independent of our knowledge of them. This principle was applied by Plato to a field which in other ways strikingly fulfilled the characteristics of reality. This is the realm of pure mathematics. Mathematical assertions and the chains of inference which are derived from them supremely display the marks of permanence, coherence, and definiteness. They are independent of the contingent circumstances of time and space; they are absolute and necessary. Plato insists that they are not inventions of our minds but fundamental constituents of reality. Nor are they abstracted from the objects of sense-perception, for they are not found in them.[1] And in very different types of experience Plato pointed to similar orders. Besides mathematical ideas there are norms of beauty and of goodness; and these too are timeless, beyond change. Thus the Ideas are not only logical principles of explanation. They are also standards of perfection.

We have seen how St. Augustine embraced these principles, deriving them in a form transmuted by religious emphasis from the writings of the Neoplatonists. And behind all the controversies of

[1] An affirmation of Realism in this field has been recently published in *A Mathematician's Apology*, by Prof. G. H. Hardy. 'I believe', he says, 'that mathematical reality lies outside us, that our function is to discover and *observe it*, and that the theorems which we prove, and which we describe grandiloquently as our 'creations' are simply our notes of our observations.'

the Middle Ages stood the belief that the principles of the world of common perception were ultimately ideal types constituted by the divine will. The controversies turned on the question whether it is possible directly to know these forms. But to the Platonic influences we must now add some features which were inherited from the fragments of Aristotle and from his Neoplatonic commentators. The chief source for the knowledge of Aristotle throughout the early Middle Ages was Boethius, and from his translations of the elementary logical treatises further distinctions were introduced into the tradition of Platonic Realism. In his logical writings Aristotle had sought to make formally explicit the principle upon which the Socratic method proceeded, and to apply it to the investigation not only of moral but of any subject of inquiry. He discussed the manner in which the essential character of things or concepts may be distinguished from inessential features. He distinguished the accidental features and the properties of a thing from its essential nature. Accidents are features which are not necessary to the being of a thing. It is not a necessary part of man that he should wear boots or be a soldier. But some features are necessary to a thing which are yet not essential to it. Such features are properties of a thing. Thus being alive is a property of man. What further can be said of an essence of a thing? It is found in those characters which uniquely distinguish the thing from other things in the same class. Thus the essence of man was found to be rationality, for it is the possession of reason which uniquely distinguishes man from other members of the class of living creatures. This point of distinction was termed a difference. The search for the universal which constituted the essence of a species was the search for a definition which expressed the difference of the species within its class or genus. We shall find these conceptions frequently recurring in the discussions which follow. The implications for medieval thought of this method of investigation were momentous.

For it was implied that the universal essence of anything, a stone or a man or piety, can only be defined in one way. It is assumed that everything possesses a fixed and definite essence. Reality is composed of a system of unalterable and ultimate entities to which are attached numerous qualities of varying degrees of relevance. Philosophical definitions are not relative. An entity, flower or heat or humanity, cannot be defined in one way at one time and in another way at another time; for this would be to deny it any essential qualities. An entity cannot be one thing at one time and another thing at the next moment; if things were in a state of continual flux knowledge would be impossible. If we are to hold to the distinction between reality and appearance, and between truth and error, we are driven to assume that everything has a determinate essence, and that there is one and only one final definition of it. And the method is ruled by the theory. The emphasis is on formal classification into species and genera. In alliance with Biblical conceptions this point of view arrested the development of natural knowledge. By supposing a vast hierarchy of qualitatively different entities it regressed from the insight of the Platonic claim for mathematics in the field of physical science. And in the realm of organisms it precluded any notion of development. But the Aristotelian logic was the mistress of exact thinking in the Middle Ages.

For the few isolated groups of scholars who were in touch by slender threads with the fragments of Greek thought, Realism was philosophy. They learnt it too from the greatest Christian philosopher, St. Augustine. Singular entities, this fever, that person, are what they are only in virtue of the common nature apprehended by thought. In reflecting on the nature of the general essences and the singular cases which reveal them, later philosophers were led to adopt positions which became the target for the shafts of Abaelard. The peculiar form of being which is enjoyed by universals was termed *subsistence* in order to distinguish it from the *existence* of physical entities. Subsistences became fundamental kinds of things side by side with individual objects. Augustinian Realism developed into an extreme Realism in which universals subsist apart from the world of particular colours and shapes and sounds. And yet they are identical essences appearing in different particular things and events. The result is that the singular features which distinguish this man or this book from others of the same species are conceived of as external and adventitious to the essences man and book. Such were some of the dangerous tendencies to which Augustinian Realism was exposed. But this extreme Realism is criticized so thoroughly by Abaelard in the passages which we are shortly to report that it is unnecessary to describe its lineaments further at this point. In modern terms what he attacked was the hypostatization of abstract ideas. Nominalism was a natural reaction to this uncompromising Realism.

But in addition to the traditional and logical sanctions which

have been touched upon there was a second influence which profoundly encouraged a Realistic interpretation of experience. The
belief that universal notions refer to independent realities found
support in the writings of the Fathers and in the rational justifica-
tion of the Faith. The study of Plato was recommended by
Clement and Origen, and the Realism of Augustine dominated the
schools until the eleventh century. We have seen how well
Platonism accorded with the Christian outlook. It envisaged a
realm of absolute, eternal and super-individual realities, arche-
types of all particular and perishing things. Christian thought
interpreted the Forms as divine Ideas, and conceived creation
after the manner of an artist and his works. The realm of Ideas was
also the realm of absolute values, a region infinitely more abiding
than anything revealed to man's senses. The approximate virtues
of the world participate in the eternal heaven of goodness. Reason
and Christian Faith met in this doctrine of the objectivity and
unity of moral judgements. And when we pass from the dogmas of
creation and of the attributes of God to other points of the Creed
we find Realistic arguments employed in their defence. They were
used in discourses on the dogma of the Trinity. If individuals and
not universals are the primary reality the doctrine of the unity of
the Godhead is endangered. If it is denied that persons are one in
virtue of their humanity, it follows that the Persons of the Trinity
do not constitute a substantial unity in virtue of their Divinity.
We shall find Anselm pressing this contention against the Nominalists. Again, Realism was applied to the most sacred practice of
religion. In the ninth century the belief had been formulated that
the consecrated elements of the Mass were transformed literally
into the body and blood of Christ. Its crudity was challenged,
notably by Berengar of Tours, and theologians, led by Lanfranc,
sought to defend the popular faith by drawing a distinction between
the real substance or universal and the accidents of bread and wine.
The real substance of the elements was transformed by the act of
the priest into the substance of the body and blood of Christ, while
the accidents or sensible appearances of the bread and wine
remained unaltered. This is the dogma of Transubstantiation.
And its theoretical basis is realistic, dependent on the distinction between universals apprehended by the understanding, and
sensible expressions of them which are inessential accidents of
real natures.

Finally, medieval social ideas were coloured with Realism.

Corporations were prior to individuals, as the universal was prior to its particulars. Dominating all activities there was the pervasive and unifying reality of the Church. And numerous institutions, the Papacy, the great monastic orders, the ecclesiastical schools, the universities, the towns, the guilds, the manors, and many other corporate personalities expressed the medieval confidence in Realist principles. In our own day there has been a portentous revival of extreme Realism in European politics.

II

Let us now return to Boethius. In the prevailing Realism of the early Middle Ages the questions which he propounded in his commentary on Porphyry provoked no serious controversy for four centuries. Yet the questions raise fundamental considerations for the traditional view of knowledge, and Boethius' own discussion of them offers suggestions which should have startled a more cultured age into discussion. The famous passage is found in the second edition of the commentary on Porphyry's Introduction.[1]

The first problem is: Do we think of species and genera as existing in the same way as objects which we perceive? Are we mistaken when we suppose that general terms, or universals, refer to real entities? Are they no more than the products of our mental processes, having no counterpart in the real world? But secondly, even if it were established that general classes exist in reality, a further and more difficult question arises. What is the nature of these entities? Everything is either material or immaterial. To which order do genus and species belong? Even though we were to succeed in answering these questions, a third problem remains. For if we were to conclude that genus and species were immaterial substances we should be driven to consider their relation to physical objects. Do they subsist with material things (*circa corpora*), or are they immaterial forms of being subsisting apart from material things (*praeter corpora*)? Boethius gives examples of each class. There are immaterial spiritual substances such as God, mind, and the soul, which can exist apart from material things. There are others, such as line, surface, and number, which cannot be separated from bodies without ceasing to be.

The first question is whether universals have being indepen-

dently of our minds. The characteristic of the general notion or
universal is that it is common to many things at once. Boethius
points out that this characteristic cannot apply to any simple single
entity. The genus, such as animal, is present in each species of men,
and present as a whole in each. But if so the genus cannot be one,
from which it follows that it is nothing existing at all. For everything which exists is a single entity. The same difficulty can be
applied to species. On the other hand, if genus is one it cannot be
common to many, for when a single thing is common to many
things it is not common to each as a whole. Each of the many
share a part of the single thing, or use it at different times. But
universals such as genera are said to be not only entirely in each
individual at the same time, but to constitute the substance of the
individuals to which they are common. Since, therefore, the universal is neither one nor many it does not exist at all.

This is a challenging conclusion. It is directed against a crude
literalism which conceived the universal as a kind of thing similar
to other existing things. Boethius now proceeds to a description of
universals in a passage wherein Aristotelian views are introduced
to his age. By the process of abstraction the mind attains ideas
which though they do not refer to real objects are not therefore
false. The mind receives from the senses a confused mass of
impressions. It has the power of uniting what is given in perception as distinct and of separating what it finds united. Thus it
apprehends the notion of a line in separation from the notion of
a body. Similarly it contemplates genera and other universals
apart from the sensible objects in which they actually inhere.
The activity of thought consists in noting the common characteristics in a number of different individuals and in comprehending
these similar features in themselves. To Porphyry's questions,
therefore, Boethius answers firstly that universals are real features
of sensible objects. They are implicitly perceived in objects, they
become explicit and intelligible through the work of the understanding. Secondly they are immaterial, though they have no
substantial existence apart from sensible things. The third question, whether universals exist independently of bodies, is thus
also answered.[1]

Boethius has turned from the interpretation of universals in a
metaphysical sense as Platonic Ideas to a psychological account of
the formation of abstract concepts. The presupposition of this

[1] C.S.E.L. xlviii. 84-5.

presupposes: substantial existence is not in form but in sensible objects!

description is that substantial existence is found not in Forms but in sensible objects. It foreshadows the Moderate Realism of the twelfth century. But it must be added that Boethius is here acting as a faithful expositor of Aristotle. He says emphatically that he himself does not hold this interpretation. In other writings he adheres to a Platonic position.

These suggestions were not pursued far in the Dark Ages. And in the centuries which succeeded the work of Boethius the theory of knowledge proposed by St. Augustine prevailed. In the eighth century Alcuin of York recommended him above all philosophers. And in the following century a great system of Neoplatonic thought was propounded by John Scotus Erigena. For him the universal is the essential reality from which the particular is derived; and it is the more real in proportion to its universality. The logical hierarchy of concepts is the scheme of reality, and the most comprehensive abstraction is the fullest Being. The eternal Forms or Ideas are in God and are expressions of the divine will. But genera and species are not true Forms. In spite of his Platonic sympathies it is doubtful whether Erigena can be termed a Realist. For the proper objects of dialectic for him are not the eternal Forms but genera and species, which are found in material things. Yet these secondary forms proceed ultimately from the true Forms.

John Scotus Erigena translated the work of 'Dionysius the Areopagite', a Christian forgery based upon the writings of the Neoplatonist, Proclus. This work continued to exercise an influence throughout the Middle Ages.

But it was not until the generation preceding that of Abaelard that the problem of the status of universals was acutely revived. Controversy was suddenly excited throughout the schools of Europe by the appearance of the unorthodox thesis of extreme Nominalism. The most prominent advocate of this heretical doctrine was Roscelin of Compiègne (1050—*circa* 1125). Unfortunately little of the writings of this original thinker have so far been discovered and we are left to infer his views from the remarks of his critics, such as St. Anselm and Abaelard.

Concepts and propositions do not express reality. What they express are various forms of assertion determined by the rules of grammar and by arbitrary meanings. Language does not express things as they are, for it names wholes of things, whereas in reality there are only indivisible sensible entities, which do not compose

the wholes named by terms. And just as it regards the distinction
of parts within an individual as purely subjective, so this theory
considers the totality of several individuals as an arbitrary collection. Accordingly, general ideas, universals, are merely names,
nomina, and even noises, *flatus vocis*. The common nature which
they assert is wholly subjective.

The theory had been advanced in Greece by many thinkers; by
Democritus, by the Sophist Gorgias, and by the Epicureans. But
for the Middle Ages it was heresy. At the basis of this Nominalism
lies an empiricist theory of knowledge. As Anslem says: 'In the
minds of these philosophers reason, which ought to be the guide
and judge of all that exists in men, is so wrapped up in material
imaginations, that it cannot extricate itself from them, nor distinguish from them those things which ought to be contemplated in
their intrinsic purity.'[1]

The lively antagonism excited by this theory was, however, less
due to its logical novelty than to the fact that it conflicted with
theological orthodoxy. It appeared, for example, to involve a
denial of the doctrine of the Trinity. Anselm warmly pointed out
that anyone who could not grasp the way in which many individual
men are one in the species man, could not admit that several
Persons are united in one God. And the man who found it difficult
to distinguish between his horse and its colour could hardly
distinguish between God and His attributes.[2] Roscelin was indicted
for Tritheism. But for our purposes the important step taken by
Roscelin was that it rejected any reference to reality in general
conceptions. *Universale est vox*. The contrast with Realism is
complete. For Realism the universal resides in the nature govern-
ing the individual. For Nominalism this unity resides only in the
common term.[3]

We shall find that in spite of the scornful language which
Abaelard uses concerning Roscelin, describing him as a *pseudo-
dialecticus* and even as a *pseudo-christianus*, his own doctrine of
universals bears the impress of the teaching he received from the
revolutionary philosopher of Compiègne. And when he passed from
the school of Roscelin to the lectures of the leading champion of
Realism, William of Champeaux, he was able to criticize his master's
position by arguments which he had learnt from Roscelin. His
attacks on Roscelin are on the ground rather of theology than of

---

[1] Anselm, *De Fide Trinitatis*, 2; P.L. clviii. 265. [2] Ib.
[3] Nominalism is treated more fully in Chapter IV.

logic; though we shall find that Abaelard departed in a significant
way from the Nominalism of his first master. Before proceeding
to unfold the manner in which he met the situation let us glance
at his character and history.

III

Peter Abaelard was born in 1079 at Pallot, near Nantes, in
Brittany. As a youth he had the singular good fortune to receive
instruction from two masters who taught opposing principles of
philosophy, Roscelin and William of Champeaux. This education
sharpened his native facility in dialectical controversy and he
displayed early the qualities of a brilliant teacher and philosopher.
His fame as a logician brought throngs of young students to his
lectures. They followed him from place to place, delighting not
only in his extraordinary skill in disputation but also in his tren-
chant way with opponents. His ruthless methods earned him the
formidable nickname of *rhinocerus indomitus*. At Paris he engaged
his former teacher, William of Champeaux, in sharp debate on the
dominant issue of the day, the problem of the status of universals;
and his resounding success excited the jealousy and suspicion of
the established schools. For many years he drew eager bands of
scholars to the slopes of St. Geneviève. Abaelard had so far directed
his impetuous but clear intellect to logical questions, but at the age
of thirty-four he suddenly deserted dialectics for theology, and put
himself to school with the most famous masters of theology in
France. But once more he soon changed the rôle of pupil for that
of rival instructor; nor did he scruple to declare his contempt for
the learning of his masters. He resumed his lectures at Paris,
discoursing now on theology as well as on philosophy. Here he met
Heloïse. The tragic story of their relations, the most famous and
the most affecting romance of the Middle Ages, has often been told.
It was succeeded by a period of profound bitterness, during which
the philosopher secluded himself in the monastery of St. Denys.
He emerged with powers enhanced. The renown of his teaching
spread through Europe. In after years a friend in writing to him
thus describes this period of his career:

'The fearful seas of the Channel were no terror to the throng of
English youths; at the sound of your name they scorned every danger,
and flocked to hear you. The distant regions of Brittany sent its savages
to be taught by you. The inhabitants of Anjou curbing their natural
brutality, came humbly to sit at your feet. Natives of Scotland, of the

Pyrenees, of Ireland; Teutons and Swabians from Normandy and Flanders were roused to fervour by your genius.'

Allowing for some amicable flattery in this description, it is manifest that Abaelard was at this time the supreme teacher of the age. From the vast concourse of students who crowded to hear him lecture at Paris or Nôgent-sur-Seine sprang the first and greatest of the medieval universities.

Meanwhile his enemies were watching. The publication of his book *On the Trinity* gave them their opportunity. A special council was called at Soissons and the book was solemnly condemned. Abaelard found himself an outcast. But the devotion of the wandering scholars would not leave him to the solitude to which he had retired. They gathered round him at Nôgent-sur-Seine, rebuilt his hut, erected a lecture hall, and established the brotherhood of the Paraclete. A few years later, on the departure of Abaelard and his pupils, the buildings were transferred to the sisterhood of which Heloïse was now a member.

After many turns of fortune, during which he narrowly escaped destruction at the hands of his enemies, Abaelard returned to Paris. Now at length he was confronted with an opponent more formidable than any whom he had faced before. Certain of his utterances had been brought to the notice of Bernard, Abbot of Clairvaux. The great religious leader was gravely disturbed by the unorthodoxy which he detected in them. A debate between Bernard and Abaelard was arranged to take place at Sens, though Bernard shrank from the prospect of meeting the great controversialist. It was Abaelard, however, who declined the contest. He appealed to Rome. The Pope, acting under the guidance of Bernard, condemned Abaelard to silence, and his disciples to excommunication. He set out to Rome to plead his cause. On the way he stayed at the Abbey of Cluny and was persuaded to remain there. For two years he was suffered to live in peace, 'allowing no moment to escape unoccupied by prayer, reading, writing, or dictation'. At the end of this period, in 1142, he died at the age of sixty-three.

There are few more impressive figures in the Middle Ages than Peter Abaelard. If he had lived four centuries later he would have been regarded as a signal example of the versatile individuality of the Renaissance. He was the pre-eminent poet of his time in secular as well as in religious verse. The self-revelation of the letters to Heloïse rivals the intimacy of the age of Cellini or

Montaigne. And the varied interests which they show, delight in the beauty of this world, in the literature of paganism, in the pleasures of life, express the very spirit of Humanism. But the main concern of Abaelard's stormy and tragic life was philosophy, and philosophy in the service of religion. 'I have no wish to be a philosopher,' he wrote to Heloïse, 'if I must abandon my allegiance to Paul; I do not desire to become Aristotle if I must separate myself from Christ.'

In addition to the *Dialectica* and other logical works he wrote an ethical dialogue, *Scito te ipsum*, in which the inward rule of conscience is vindicated, even though God should appear to enjoin otherwise. An early theological work, the celebrated *Sic et Non*, is a collection of contradictory statements to be found in the Bible and the Fathers. It was composed in order to stimulate students to exercise their wits upon the problems of theology.

Abaelard composed a number of treatises on logic in the course of which the problem of universals is discussed at length. These treatises consist, for the most part, of commentaries on the works of Porphyry and of Boethius. From these writings we may select for consideration portions of two commentaries known from their opening words as the *Logica ingredientibus*, 'Logic for Beginners', and the *Logica nostrorum petitioni sociorum*, 'Written in response to the request of our friends'.[1] We are to follow somewhat closely his discussion in these treatises. They are valuable sources for the philosophical interests of the beginning of the twelfth century, for Abaelard is at pains to describe carefully the theories which he is attacking. In the vigorous and often sardonic criticism to which he subjects the orthodox views we hear an echo of the challenging methods of the *rhinocerus indomitus* and catch a glimpse of the eager crowded debates at Nôtre Dame or Nôgent.

IV

Abaelard introduces the discussion by recalling Porphyry's questions. He had inquired, in the first place, whether universals, such as man, animal, rose, exist apart from the mind that conceives them. Are they no more than mental operations? Secondly, if it is found that universal entities actually exist, that rose in general is a form of being not dependent on the mental process that apprehends

[1] The texts are to be found in *Beiträge zur Geschichte der Philosophie des Mittelalters*, Band xxi (1919), edited by Dr. Bernhard Geyer, pp. 1–32 and 505–83. The references which follow give the pages of the text in the *Beiträge*.

it, what is the nature of these forms of being? Are they material or immaterial substances? Thirdly, the problem of their relation to the objects perceived by the senses arises. Do they exist apart from sensible objects or are they united with them? To these questions of Porphyry, Abaelard adds a further inquiry concerning the relation between the individual instances and the universal term. If the objects to which the general name refers were abolished, could the universal retain a meaning for thought? For example, could the generic term rose continue to have significance if no particular roses were to exist?[1]

These problems are approached by means of a survey of current doctrines. The main division is between those philosophers who hold that universals are only words (*voces*) and those who maintain that they refer also to things (*res*). And since genera and species are acknowledged to be universals, we are invited to inquire into the nature of universals by an examination of these types. At the outset it is necessary to be agreed upon the general meaning of the terms universal and particular. Here Abaelard cites the accepted Aristotelian definition. A universal is that which refers to many items at once, *quod de pluribus natum est aptum praedicari*. It embraces a number of different particulars; flower refers to all types and colour and shapes of flowers. A particular or an individual, according to Porphyry, is asserted only of one item. We shall find that these traditional definitions are strictly adhered to during the discussion. Abaelard next cites the main authorities. Aristotle and Porphyry state that universals are things, but Aristotle in another passage, and Boethius, assert that they are names or terms, *nomina*. They are said to be signs of the way in which things are determined. If this latter version were accepted we should be obliged to deny that universals are species in the realist sense, for a term is not a substantial thing but an accident. Yet terms can be accepted as universals, for they can be asserted of many things. This interpretation, for which he here claims high authority, is, in fact, close to Abaelard's own position; and he anticipates his conclusion in the phrase that words which are universal terms perform the function of predicates of propositions.[2]

The first school of contemporary thought to be considered is the teaching of emphatic Realism. It is the doctrine that universals are kinds of object, existing independently of the mind. What is the meaning of this account? How can any thing, or even a

[1] p. 8.   [2] pp. 9-10.

collection of things, be asserted of many things? This house, and
Socrates, are instances of things. How can they be asserted of
many things? How can universals be things? Let us consider by
what arguments this theory is defended.[1]

The view that universals are *res* holds that they are the substantial essences manifested in a number of particular instances, the
particular instances differing from one another only in their forms,
that is to say, in their special natures. The universal essence of a
class of things, such as men, is one; it assumes variety by becoming
embodied in forms of differing degrees of particularity. Now,
consider the logic of this position. If these particular modifications of the identical substance were removed there would be no
difference whatsoever between particular things. All things would
be the same. 'Man', for example, is the single material essence of
both Plato and Socrates. The modifications of the identical substance in virtue of which Plato and Socrates are individuals with
different characteristics are accidents. These individual characteristics may be present or absent without affecting the essence of
man. So, too, creatures which differ in kind are presumed to
be expressions of the essential and identical substance, animal.
The different kinds of animals are derived by assuming that a
number of accidental differences have been introduced into the
identical substance. This substance is like a piece of wax that can
be moulded into many shapes; though the analogy is not precise,
since the material of the universal substance remains the same in
all the models which are made from it. The universal, then, becomes individual by means of external, adventitious forms. In the
language of this school, it is said to *subsist* in itself naturally or in
reality, apart from its forms, but to *exist* actually, through the
forms or physical expressions of it. The real subsistence of the
universal can be apprehended only by pure thought or understanding, *intellectus*, untouched by sense-perception. And thought
apprehends it as immaterial and absolute.[2]

Such is Abaelard's summary of extreme Realism. The doctrine
was endowed, as we have seen, with high sanction. And, as he
here observes, it was the dominant theory of the time. He makes
no mention of the arguments from which it drew its strength. He
describes only the conclusion which it reaches, that genuine substances are principles apprehended in general ideas. And these
realities that underlie the changing and manifold objects of percep-

[1] p. 10.   [2] pp. 10–11.

tion retain their identity unaffected by change and difference. In this Platonic and Augustinian citadel of thought Abaelard, for the first time, makes a formidable breach.

His first criticism of the doctrine is that it destroys all distinctions between things. The doctrine implies that one thing is in essence the same as another thing, however different its special forms may be. Consequently a rational animal will be the same in essence as an irrational animal. Two individuals, in fact, possessing contrary or incompatible qualities will be fundamentally the same. And this contravenes the rule that contrary qualities cannot exist at the same time in the same thing. It is true that some qualities that appear to be incompatible may occur in the same substance without being really incompatible. Thus 'great' and 'small' can both be present in the same thing at the same time. The thing is great in one respect and small in another. But this explanation does not apply to qualities such as rationality and irrationality. These are genuinely incompatible.[1]

It may be said that, in spite of this contradiction, these qualities are actually found existing together in the same individual, for example, in Socrates. But if they are both in Socrates at the same time, they must be not only in Socrates but also in an ass at the same time. For, in this philosophy, Socrates and the ass are fundamentally the same being; both are, in essence, animal. Whatever is present in Socrates apart from the peculiar and accidental characteristics of Socrates is identical with what is present in the ass apart from the accidental characteristics of the ass. The features that make the ass Socrates and Socrates the ass are essential features. The individual differences between them are external and accidental.[2] The force of the argument rests, in part, upon the sharp division assumed in medieval thought between man and other animals. An ass could not be rational. Yet on this theory it inevitably follows that it is. But the main point is that by making individual differences adjectival or superficial, everything becomes everything else and clear thinking becomes impossible.

Some realists, he proceeds, seek to escape these conclusions by affirming that the difficulties are verbal. No real contradiction is involved in saying that a rational animal is also an irrational animal. Certainly the words refer to the same thing, namely, animal. But they signify that it is rational in one respect and irrational in another. They refer in fact, not to the thing's essence,

---

[1] p. 11. [2] pp. 11–12, 515.

but to its forms or specific features. And forms, since they are relative and accidental, may occur together without conflicting. There is no contradiction in such propositions as 'a rational animal is a mortal animal' and 'a white animal is an animal which walks'. Rationality and mortality, whiteness and walking, are not mutually exclusive terms; each pair of terms may qualify a subject at the same time without contradiction. Otherwise one might as well say that no animal is man because nothing, in so far as it is animal, is man.[1] In this way the identity of substances may be defended in spite of the presence in them of contrary forms.

But Abaelard rejects this argument, not by insisting further on the incompatibility of some forms in a substance which is presumed to be identical, but by denying that forms can serve to distinguish particular expressions of substance. For they too dissolve into identity. His reasoning here is based on the Aristotelian doctrine of categories. There are ten modes into which things may be fundamentally classified. Substance, quantity, quality, relation are examples of these fundamental classifications. Now substance is presupposed by all the other categories. Variety is due to the forms by which the substantial and general characters are made particular. But since each of the categories expresses essence or substance all instances of them are fundamentally identical. Two individuals, Socrates and Plato, contain in themselves characteristics belonging to each of the categories. Since each of these features are fundamentally the same all the forms of one are also forms of the other. Forms, therefore, do not serve to distinguish individuals any more than substances distinguish them. For they too dissolve into substance.[1]

Abaelard does not scruple to bring a charge of heresy against the doctrine. For if it be admitted, it would follow that the divine substance which excludes all forms is identical with physical substance, that is to say, primary matter, which also excludes them.[2] This ingenious accusation of pantheism must have sorely tried William of Champeaux. And further difficulties are pressed with inexhaustible persistence. We need not describe them all here. He concludes this part of his examination by reiterating the point that the differences between individuals cannot rest upon accidents. The qualities that constitute the nature of a thing must be intrinsic to its nature, not external features of it. And if these qualities constitute the nature of a thing they must be universals.

[1] p. 12.   [2] p. 515.

The suggestion here is that there is a manifold variety of independent substances.[1]

The doctrine that universality lies in a metaphysical identity which is the essential nature of things has been rejected. Abaelard now turns to examine the teaching of a more recent variety of Realism, a version which in his view comes nearer to the truth than the theory which he has so far been discussing. This type of Realism is known as the doctrine of *indifference*. We have notices that it was the doctrine which William of Champeaux was driven to uphold in the face of Abaelard's criticisms of orthodox Realism. This theory departs so far from Realism as to accept a pluralist basis of knowledge. Individual things not only differ from one another in their forms, the features which distinguish them in their species, but are substantially distinct existences. What exists in one thing does not in any way exist in another thing, whether it be a point of matter (the uniform underlying substance of things) or of form (the determinate expression). If these differences were not ultimate we should be led into an infinite regress; we should be obliged to refer the different forms or essences to more fundamental forms or essences, and so *ad infinitum*. But this school of thought while holding that all things are fundamentally distinct from one another, contrive at the same time to believe in universals. How do they reconcile this belief with their pluralist principles? They teach that things which are distinct are yet the same not essentially but *indifferently*, that is to say in so far as they are not different. The upshot of this view is that the same thing may be described as universal or particular according to the way in which it is taken. Things have universal characteristics in so far as they share the same characteristics. Individual men are man in so far as they resemble one another. They are individual and particular in so far as they differ from one another.

Abaelard's examination of this position relies upon a literal adherence to the preliminary definitions. These philosophers say that individuals are themselves universals in virtue of their similarity to other individuals. Similar individuals, let us say trees, are referred to as classes or universals, not because they are in essence universals, but because numbers of individuals are like them. But this conflicts with the definition of individual, namely, that it is one, not many. One thing taken by itself cannot resemble anything else. And how is it possible on this theory to distinguish between

---

[1] p. 13.

a universal and a particular by reference to predication ? For in the
same way in which 'man' expresses the common features of
numbers of particular men, an individual such as Socrates also
resembles many men. Certainly man in so far as he is man, and
Socrates in so far as he is man, resembles others. But neither man
in so far as he is Socrates, nor Socrates in so far as he is Socrates,
resembles others. On this view 'man' and 'Socrates' are defined in
the same way. Universals and particulars are not therefore distinguished.[1]

The general entity man which is in Socrates and the individual
Socrates himself refer to the same being ; just as Socrates is at the
same time white and a grammarian. But though these characteristics are in him, they are not different from him. The fact that he
is white or a grammarian cannot be distinguished from himself. It
is said that Socrates resembles Plato in the fact of being man. But
men differ from one another both in matter and form. As himself
Socrates is different from Plato. The phrase 'resemblance in the
fact of man' is taken by some authorities in a negative sense, to
imply that Socrates does not differ from Plato in being man. Here
Abaelard is recording the reply made by William of Champeaux
to his own earlier criticisms. It is certainly not a happy contribu-
tion to the debate. It is like saying, he caustically observes, that
Socrates does not differ from Plato in being stone, since neither is a
stone. If the proposition is taken affirmatively, that they do not
differ in being man, it is false. For if Socrates does differ from
Plato in being man, he does not differ from him in himself. If
he differs in himself from him, while he is himself the thing which
is man, he must also differ from himself in the same respect.[1]

In the discussion over universals philosophers were fond of using
the phrases 'in so far as', or 'to the extent of'. Abaelard finds
them ambiguous and confusing. As an aid towards a clearer definition of the universal or of the particular, such limiting phrases are
useless. In place of the definition 'the genus is that which refers to
many things' is substituted the definition 'the genus, to the extent
of being a genus, refers to many'. This phrase throws no further
light upon the nature of genus ; it merely repeats the subject which
is to be defined. And so when it is said that men are identical in so
far as they are men, the question remains what nature and status
this identity possesses. Moreover, how is it possible on this theory
to distinguish between the genus or universal and the individual ?

The genus is defined as that which refers to many. But the individual is also said to be universal in this sense. An individual man is said also to be man, and even animal. These philosophers attempt to distinguish between the two on the ground that genus in its capacity of being individual is excluded from this definition. But the description is not applied to the genus nor to the individual absolutely (*simpliciter*) but only 'in respect of being' genus, and 'in respect of being' individual. They are not, therefore, distinguished, since what is asserted concerning genus can be with equal truth asserted of the individual, for both refer, in an absolute sense, to the same thing. It is impossible, in fact, to combine a clearly distinct and a relative sense of the terms universal and particular; and this is what the Indifference theory tries to do.

Again, it is said that the proposition 'a man is walking' is false for the species, but true for the particular. How can this distinction be maintained if the same thing is both species and particular? It is replied that the universal man in so far as it is universal does not walk. This is like saying 'a man, in so far as he is an animal, does not have a head'. It could equally well be said that a particular man in so far as he is a particular man has no head, nor walks; or that, in so far as a being is rational, it is not mortal.[1] But there are conflicts of opinion within this school of thought, and Abaelard proceeds to discuss a further interpretation of the general doctrine which seeks to combine a belief in the uniqueness of things with an acceptance of their universality. One party maintained this position by proclaiming the doctrine of *collectio*. A universal is no more than a collection of things. Individuals such as Socrates or Plato are not species in themselves; all individual men taken together constitute the species man, all individual animals collected into one unit form the genus animal. Another group of philosophers combined this interpretation of the universal with the view discussed above. They asserted that a species is not only the collection of individuals, but is also in an individual in so far as it is also universal. When these philosophers say that the particular object Socrates is asserted of many they intend the description to be taken in a figurative sense as meaning many are the same as he, or he has qualities which correspond with those of other men. Consequently, they postulate as many species and genera as there are individuals, but according to the similarity between different things they assume a smaller number of universals.[2]

[1] Cf. p. 37.   [2] p. 14.

Against the view that universals are collections of things Abaelard brings the following objections. How can the mass of men taken as one, he asks, be asserted of many? If what is meant is that the whole is asserted part by part of many different things, so that distinct portions of the whole refer to different things, then the doctrine has no bearing on the nature of universals, as ordinarily understood, that nature which the doctrine professes to explain. For universals are understood to be pervasive, that is to say, they exist wholly in each individual. The relation of the universal to individuals does not consist in the relation of parts to a whole, as parts of a field are shared between different persons. On this interpretation any individual, such as Socrates, would be a universal since it includes many parts. And any group of men would constitute a universal or a species. Any type of material or mental collection of entities would be a universal substance. A combination of collections of substances would constitute a supreme genus or class. If one group were taken away, the remaining groups, since they formed a total, would form a supreme class. Consequently groups could be classified in different ways to form a supreme class. But (Abaelard appeals to an accepted principle of logic) there cannot be any number of supreme genera. It may be replied that no collection of things which is included under the supreme genus is itself a supreme genus. But it is still true that when one collection or substance is taken away from the total collection of substances, if the remaining collection is not the supreme genus, it must be a species. For it is a universal. And if it is a species it must possess a correlative species under its genus. What could this be? For there would be no other collection to form a species.

Further, every universal is said to be prior in nature to its individuals of which it is composed. Again a collective whole and a universal are traditionally distinguished thus; in a collection the part is different from the whole, in a universal the species is the same as the genus, in the sense that the genus is implicit in the species. But how can the total number of men constitute the aggregate of animals?[1] For these reasons the doctrine that the universal is a collection of things must be put aside.

Abaelard has now concluded the first part of his discussion. What is the significance of the series of criticisms which we have been following? Contemporary philosophic thought was preoccu-

[1] p. 15.

pied with the problem of the meaning of general terms, for reasons
which we here outlined above. The identity of characteristics in
things was considered to be a fundamental kind of thing. General
terms referred to types of real being. These types of reality are
immanent in all the particular instances which are comprehended
in the universal term, in all reds and men. But the cardinal point
of this theory was that the particular instances are inessential
features of these realities. The particular reds, the individual men,
are accidents. They are appearances, expressions of realities whose
nature is utterly different from them. For these realities are
general; and they are the only genuine realities. It is these assertions of Realism, that individuals are radically distinct from
universals and that individuals are unreal, which Abaelard merci-
lessly assails. He exposes the monistic consequences of the doctrine; everything would, in the end, be everything else. He
unmasks its contradictions; the multiplicity of things is traced to
the presence of accidents, yet there are said to be many immaterial
substances. And he exhibits the confusions into which defenders
of the doctrine were led by such resorts as the Indifference theory,
and the interpretation of universals as an assemblage of particulars.
The positive outcome of his assault on these types of Realism is
that the manifold variety of things is not an illusion. The negative
result is the destruction of extreme Realism. By the former conclusion a more careful restatement of Realism was made necessary in
closer sympathy with Aristotelian conceptions, in which the empirical aspects of experience should be recognized. The intimate
association of Realism with the principles of Faith is a measure of
Abaelard's achievement in criticism. It is not to be wondered at
that the rumours of his onslaught stirred Europe and drew throngs
of earnest scholars to the lectures on the slopes of St. Geneviève.
Far-reaching changes in philosophy were due; Abaelard's attacks
on the incautious Realism prevalent in his day opened men's
minds for the renaissance of Aristotelian thought in the thirteenth
century.

V

Abaelard now turns to the second part of the inquiry into
contemporary theories of universals. The theories that remain to
be considered assert that universals are not things but words. But
Nominalism is not treated in the critical vein in which Realism has
been approached. The extreme form advocated by Roscelin, that

universals are *voces*, mere words, is repudiated. It is simply pointed out that words express meaning, and the discussion passes on to analyse the meaning of terms. This leads to an account of Abaelard's own theory in which the problems of universals find solution.

He turns, as is usual with him, to consider language. In what way can words function as universals? The grammarians name certain terms *appellative* and others *proper*. The former refer to a general class, the latter to individuals. In a parallel way, philosophers name certain elementary forms of discourse (*sermones*) universals, and others particulars. A universal word is one which is designed to be predicated as a single word of many items at once. The term 'man' can be united to the particular names of many men. A particular word can be referred to one subject only, such as the word 'Socrates', so long as it indicates one particular person. But, Abaelard points out, grammatical parallels will not take us far. The construction of sentences in which the philosopher is concerned are different operations. The grammarian is occupied with the formal conjunction of any nominative term with another term by means of the copula 'is'. The philosopher is interested in the meaning of sentences. He is concerned with the status of the objects to which terms refer. No error of grammar is contained in the proposition 'man is a stone'; in philosophy the statement is inadmissible.[1]

He now attacks the problem directly. Let us, he says, carefully investigate the property of universal words. It is a matter of some difficulty. They do not appear to refer to anything, nor to give a clear conception of anything. The universal 'man' does not apply to any definite person, nor, as we have seen, to the whole body of men. We have noticed that certain philosophers suppose that universal terms refer to the individual in so far as he is man. If in fact Socrates alone is sitting in this house, then the proposition 'a man is sitting in this house' is true. But the universal term 'man' does not necessarily designate Socrates. Otherwise we could infer from the proposition that the man sitting in this house was Socrates. To what, then, do universal terms refer?[2]

General terms, it is insisted, are not, as the Nominalists averred, merely words, but refer to general notions. The word 'man' is a name given to individuals in virtue of an element which is common to many individuals. If we are to avoid a return to Realism we must examine this common principle more closely. Is the term called common because of a common nature in which different things share? Or is the common character imputed to things by the mind? Or is it due to both principles?[1]

The common or general nature to which universal terms refer calls first for consideration. Individual men are distinct from one another both in form and essence. But they are united in the fact that they are men. Now this does not mean that different men are united in the entity man. No such entity exists. In saying that individuals are united in being man the words do not refer to any essence. The nature of man or of any universal (he is never tired of insisting) is not a thing. What, then, is it? He terms it a *status*, which we may translate 'a thing's nature in the order of things'. The common principle in virtue of which the universal term is attached to things is to be found in the fact that individual things can be grouped together in thought on the basis of identical features; but the groups are not also real objects, still less essences. Identity is a relation between things. The common features which are discerned in different men belong indeed to the real nature of men. The mind apprehends these common qualities through the process of forming conceptions.

This position, in admitting a common nature in things, is so far realist, though Abaelard is anxious not to identify this nature with the transcendent object of the extreme realists. But let us follow his further explanations. The key to the problem he finds in a psychological analysis of the processes of knowledge. He turns from metaphysical inquiries concerning the common nature to which concepts refer to discuss the operation of conceiving itself. He sketches the components of knowledge in the following terms.

Sense-perception and pure thought (*intellectus*) are sharply distinguished from one another. Both perception and thought are activities of the mind. But perception is exercised through bodily instruments, and senses perceive only bodies and what are in them. Thought does not require a bodily instrument and in consequence does not need a physical object. It is satisfied with the image of a thing. The mind forms this representation for itself, directing the activity of its intelligence upon it. I perceive a tower standing in the plain. If the tower is removed sense-perception vanishes with it but thought remains, since the tower's likeness is retained by

[1] p. 19.

the mind. So far this account conforms with Augustine's theory.
The mind forms its material from within itself receiving no aid
from the body. Abaelard now points out that the act of thought
must be distinguished from its object, just as the process of perceiving is not identical with the object perceived. Thought is an
activity of the mind, in virtue of which it is said to understand.
But before the act of understanding can take place the process of
imagination must intervene. The understanding is directed on an
imaginary and fictitious object which the mind constructs for itself
whenever it wishes to do so and in any way it desires. Such
representations resemble the imaginary countries seen in a dream
or the form of a building which a craftsman is in course of design-
ing. He conceives in his mind an ideal image of the work to be
achieved.[1] In a word thought is free to construct its own objects.

Abaelard emphasizes these distinctions because he found that
some philosophers tended to identify thinking and its objects.
They called the image of the tower the same as the thought of the
tower. He rejects this subjective idealism. The image is a likeness
of the thing. And this is the proper object of thought. But if we
stop at this point we have not reached true knowledge. Real
qualities, the squareness and height of the tower, exist only in
bodies. Conceptual thinking cannot be formed from fictitious
qualities. We may say that the image in a mirror to which sight
seems to refer is in reality nothing, since it is clear that in the white
surface of the mirror a contrary quality often appears.[2] Conceiving
is not like this. It refers to reality. Something more than an
image which may turn out to be fictitious is required. The understanding operates on the image so as to apprehend the nature of
objects.[3] Here we have a dim foreshadowing of St. Thomas's
account.

Thinking, then, is an activity directed upon an image, and the
mind can form images at will. We have now to distinguish between
thoughts which are directed to universals and those which are
applied to particulars. Now the universal term refers to a generalized and confused image of a number of things, while the particular term calls up one only. When I hear the word 'man' an image
arises in my mind which is so related to individual men that it is
common to all of them, specific to none. When, however, I hear
the word 'Socrates', the likeness of a definite person arises in my
mind. The common form to which a universal term refers is the

[1] p. 20.   [2] p. 21.   [3] Cf. p. 317.

generalized image of many individuals, like a painting of a lion, which does not portray the characteristics of any particular lion, but a typical lion.[1]

The conclusion which Abaelard has now reached, that universals consist of generalized images, is an unfortunate one. The position is exposed to the criticism which Berkeley afterwards levelled against Locke. It is an inadequate description of the manner in which the mind comes to form general conceptions. In coming to understand what is meant by 'lion' we do not put together all pictures of lions which we have seen and produce in our minds a composite picture. Still less do we mean by the universal 'lion' any form of image. Our philosopher is struggling to produce a theory of abstraction upon the basis of particular images.

In a later passage he proceeds farther into the psychology of the matter. Now matter and form are always found in combination, but reason has the power of contemplating now matter by itself, now form. And it may conceive of them in combination. In the two former activities the mind is abstracting. It abstracts an element from a complex object for the purpose of considering its nature. The third instance is one of synthesis. But it also supposes abstraction. For example, the substance of this man is body and animal and man, and it is clothed with infinite forms. So long as I restrict myself to the material essence of the substance ignoring all other forms, I have a concept of abstraction. Again when I attend only to its physical quality, combining it with the substance, this concept is also formed by abstraction, although it involves some process of synthesis compared with the former abstractions, for it considers the physical quality as well as the substance. But other forms, such as life, sensation, reason, whiteness, I ignore.[2]

Conceptions of this kind are considered by some philosophers to be misleading and vain for the reason that they apprehend an object in a way which does not relate to its real nature. We can think of matter and of form separately; but neither in reality exist separately. The process of abstraction, however, does not misconceive the object. When I consider this man from the point of view only of substance, ignoring the fact that he is also animal and man and a grammarian, I am not thinking of anything which is not really in the man: though I am not apprehending all that is in him. And when I say that I am considering only one quality of the real object,

[1] p. 22.   [2] p. 25.

the emphasis is on the way in which the object is looked at, not to
the way in which it really exists. The abstract quality is not in
reality the only character of the thing. The act of thought takes it
as the only character. The quality is conceived separately from
other qualities, not as though it existed in reality separated from
them. Sense-perception, indeed, often operates in the same manner
in relation to composite objects. If an image consists partly of
gold, partly of silver, I can turn my attention now to the gold
aspect, now to the silver.[1]

The act of conceiving universals, therefore, always presumes a
process of abstraction. It is a partial view of many individuals.
When I hear the word 'men' or 'whiteness' or 'white', the import
of the word is not the whole of any object. The term 'man'
provides me with the ideas of animal and rational mortals, not
with the idea of particular individuals. The content of the general
idea (he persists in holding) is a general composite image. A very
important point is now mentioned. Universals are involved in the
conception even of an individual. In the consciousness of 'this
man' the abstract character is perceived in the particular instance.
This is the basis of Abaelard's view, and requires more explanation
than it receives here. It implies a rejection of the theory of
universalia post rem, the theory of the Nominalists. But the implications which point to a distinction between substantive universals
and abstract universals are not developed. The former unify our
impressions in the object as perceived and recognized; the latter
unify qualities of many objects. The text, however, goes on to
justify Porphyry's description of universals as *sola, nuda,* and *pura*.
They are separate from sense-perception, empty of specific characters and free from reference to any thing.[2]

VI

Abaelard is now in a position to answer Porphyry's questions.
The first question was whether universals are real entities existing
independently of the mind which conceives them. The question
raises the postulate of Realism. Abaelard's reply is that universal
terms refer indeed to reality. They do not refer to nothing at
all as the extreme Nominalists maintain. Yet in a certain sense
universals exist only for thought. For they embrace abstract not
concrete views of things. Confusion has arisen over this question
only because a false dilemma has been presented. The question has

[1] p. 25.   [2] p. 28.

been taken to imply that universals are either real or not real, or that they either exist wholly in the mind or do not so exist. But the truth does not lie with these alternatives.

The second question was whether universals are material or immaterial entities. Abaelard demurs to the terms of the question. He observes acutely that the alternatives are better expressed in terms of what is discrete or locally distinct and what is not discrete. Every existent thing is discrete. In this sense universals are material in the fact that they refer to real discrete objects, immaterial in respect to the way in which they conceive these objects. Thought takes objects, or rather features of objects, together though they are perceived as distinct entities.

The answer to the third and critical problem whether or not universals are found in sensible objects or apart from them follows from the answers given to the previous questions. There are three ways in which immaterial entities may be related to sensible objects. They may exist only in sensible objects; mind is given as an instance of this type. They may be found in connexion with sensible objects, without being distinct existences. In this case, of which whiteness is an example, they are said to subsist in the sensible things. Finally there are some immaterial entities which exist entirely apart from sensible objects, such as the divine spirit and the soul.

Now Realist philosophers maintain that universals subsist in the sensible objects in the sense that they are substances inherent in objects which are sensible in virtue of external forms attached to substances. These substances can subsist in reality apart from the sensible object. Accordingly genera and species are traditionally described as being apprehensible by thought apart from them. Here the real nature of genera and species are considered by reason as continuing to subsist by themselves even when the external forms through which the senses become aware of them have been removed. Universals, according to this view, are both in sensible objects and at the same time continue to have being outside them. It is from this standpoint that the third question was raised. But Abaelard does not accept this position, except in so far as universals may have real being in the divine mind. A universal term does not point to any kind of sensible object, for this is the function of perception. And the objects of perception are the only kind of objects which possess genuine reality for human thought. Yet because universals are elicited from perceived objects they may be described as being in them; while they can equally well be termed non-sensible in so far as they are due to the activity of the mind.

And to the further question whether universals could continue to exist if there were no particulars, Abaelard returns an emphatic negative. For if their particulars were to vanish universals could not refer to many things. Yet the universal would still have meaning for thought, in spite of being deprived of particular reference. Otherwise the negative proposition 'there is no rose' could not be expressed.[1]

He concludes by pointing to the principal source of confusion in the discussions, the confusion between words and the things to which they refer. When the significance of terms is under discussion the argument is apt to move from words to objects and from objects to words. This ambiguity in logic as well as in grammar leads many into error. They fail to grasp that it is the function of terms to be applied to things in various ways, and they suppose that they are treating of things when they are treating of logical terms.[2]

Universals, then, are neither *voces* nor *res*, neither words nor things. Here Abaelard introduces his own modification of the Nominalism of Roscelin. Universals are *sermones*, concepts. The *vox* of Roscelin is a mere physical occurrence, a displacement of air. But the word means something. The word 'flower' is not merely a physical event; it refers to a general nature. But this general nature is arbitrarily selected. The human mind imposes itself upon the natural order as a sculptor fashions the stone to form a statue. Universal terms, *sermones*, imply a judgement about things, the judgement, namely that many different things have common qualities.[3]

The entities to which universal words refer are genuine through abstract properties of things. General conceptions are derived from the nature of things as they exist. Thought cannot grasp the concrete and total being of classes of objects. The *modus intelligendi* falls short of the *modus subsistendi*.[4] But by its conceptions the mind is enabled to grasp cross-sections of the manifold data of experience. These aspects are similarities discerned in a number of different individuals and contemplated in detachment from them. The universal man does not present to the mind a metaphysical reality to which individual men owe their being. It registers the observation that men are alike in being men.

[1] p. 30.   [2] pp. 30–2.   [3] p. 522; cf. p. 323.   [4] p. 25.

The position is now clear. The activity of thought isolates features which are common to a number of particular objects or events and attends to them as separate entities. These entities, whiteness, substance, rose, are genuine aspects of the discrete objects perceived by the senses. But they are not forms of being distinct from objects. In thinking the mind breaks up the complex detail of the concrete world and refashions it into objects of thought. The doubtful doctrine of the generalized image is improved by the notion of *sermo*, logical construction. And this process of analysis and synthesis is implicit in knowledge of particulars. Sense and thought co-operate fundamentally in all experience. When the mind perceives, general ideas are already implicitly present.[1]

The doctrine takes discrete individual things as real and as the point from which knowledge starts. Concepts are formed from an acquaintance with objects. Knowledge begins with particulars and progresses to the general. But this is not to move away from particulars to a separate realm of being. Theological thought was too deeply based upon Augustine for Abaelard to offer no acknowledgements to the Platonic Ideas. Ideas exist as patterns of things in the divine mind. But his theory of human knowledge is Aristotelian. The understanding knows ideas by abstracting them from things; and abstract knowledge must refer to the details of perception. ' Intellectus per abstractionem divisim attendit, non divisa, alioquin cassus esset.' Thought in virtue of its power of abstraction apprehends separate aspects of objects. It does not suppose these features to be distinct entities; for since there are no such entities it would be void of content.

VII

Abaelard's position has often been described as Conceptualism. This term indicates a qualified form of Nominalism. Those philosophers in medieval and modern times who have adopted Conceptualism are at one with the Nominalists in denying that there are any universal realities. But they admit that general notions of concepts provide the content of thinking. Concepts, however, are constructions of our minds. They are arbitrarily framed according to our purposes by a process of abstraction from particular impressions, such impressions being our sole genuine contact with the external world. Partial aspects of separate perceived items are selected and

[1] p. 95.

grouped into unities, man, green, goodness; the other features in the complex perceived individual being ignored. The abstract entities are fixed by language and exist for our minds as independent objects of thought. We argue about them as though they corresponded to real facts. On this view universals are derived entirely from the mind.

This position certainly corresponds with much that Abaelard asserts in the latter part of the passage we have been following. His interest in the process of abstraction instead of in the metaphysical problem has a decided conceptualist note. It presumes that things are known in perception prior to universalizing them. Relations as well as general ideas appear to be arbitrary. He speaks of conceiving a common likeness and of imposing general terms on things in virtue of this conception. If these and similar phrases comprised his view he would assuredly be exposed to the charge of Conceptualism which is brought against him by historians of medieval philosophy. For Conceptualism (at any rate of this order) is a plainly inadequate account of the nature of universals. It begs the question. Before the mind can abstract a common element from its experience of different individuals it must judge that they possess it. In order to construct the ideas of man, blue or shape, we have to notice similar elements in a variety of men, blue objects, and things with form. We may arbitrarily select this or that common quality, but the common quality must be already there distributed among numerous different entities; it cannot be a pure invention of our minds. There are indeed many difficulties here. But such a minimum of Realism seems to be necessary to account not merely for the relevance of thinking, but even of perceiving. For an individual object, a dog or a pen, is an implicit universal. As has been shown often in the history of thought the mind could never be aware of a train of mere particulars. But these considerations will be developed further when we come to examine the Nominalism and Conceptualism of William of Ockham.

Now, Abaelard clearly admits the minimum of Realism to which we have referred. He insists against Roscelin that the process of abstraction does not necessarily falsify our knowledge of the object. Universals are grounded in the nature of things. Man or green or Divinity are not mere sounds nor mental figments. 'Universal terms are both corporeal in respect to the nature of things'—that is to say greenness or humanity are actual features of things—'and incorporeal in respect to their meaning'—for they refer to general qualities artificially isolated from individual things. Universals are faithful representations of reality, but they are partial aspects, never reaching the concreteness of perception. This is not Conceptualism. It is an early expression of Moderate Realism.

In seeking for a middle way between a Realism that severed the universal from the particular, and a Nominalism which abolished meaning, Abaelard is led to find reality in the field of individual objects. Universals are derivative. Not that he was any friend to empirical methods in the modern sense. 'The discerning man', he says, 'is he who has the ability to grasp and ponder the hidden causes of things. And by hidden causes I mean those which concern the origin of things. These must be investigated more by reason than by practical experiments.'[1] This is an utterance typical of the medieval view of knowledge.

Yet it must be admitted that Abaelard is happier in exposing the difficulties of contemporary Realism, in ridiculing verbalism and the hypostatization of general terms, than in working out a satisfactory theory of abstraction and of the universal. This task was left to St. Thomas, who was aided by a wider acquaintance with the works of Aristotle. But already before Abaelard's death the logical treatises were being circulated and studied. We obtain a comprehensive picture of philosophical opinion on the problem of universals shortly after the time of Abaelard from a passage in the *Metalogicon* of the Englishman, John of Salisbury. John is one of the most agreeable figures in medieval literature. But scholarship was not his main concern. He was adviser to kings and archbishops and played a conspicuous part in the ecclesiastical politics of twelfth-century England. In his student days he attended for a brief period the lectures of Abaelard at Paris. His principal works were dedicated to his friend and master, Thomas Becket. The main purpose of the *Metalogicon* is to recommend the study of Aristotle's logic, but it throws a most interesting light on the intellectual life of the time. In the second book John describes the various schools of thought on the question of universals.[2] (The work was finished in the year 1159.) A few philosophers still maintain the theory of Roscellinus that universals consist of words (*voces*), though this extreme Nominalism almost disappeared with its author. The view of Abaelard, that universals are judgements (*sermones*), finds adherents, and John hails those who adopt this

[1] p. 506.   [2] *Metalogicon*, ii. 17, ed. C. C. J. Webb, Oxford, 1929

position as his friends. But he thinks they have sadly distorted
the teaching. They think it incredible that a thing can be predicated of another thing, in spite of the fact that Aristotle is the
author of this incredible doctrine. Another school holds that
genera and species are intellectual principles in the mind, an
opinion which springs from Cicero and Boethius. These innate
principles they call 'notions'. Turning to the Realists John finds
that those who think that universals are realities comprise many
divisions of belief. Some say that because everything that exists
must be a single entity, universals must be single entities. But
they allow that distinct substantial universals can be united in
essence, putting forward the doctrine of *status*. John says, however, that this view is not now held. A further party follows
Bernard of Chartres in asserting the Platonic theory of Ideas, in the
sense that universals are counterparts of eternal realities. This
view, that universals are supersensible realities, is not wholly alien
to the teaching of Aristotle, and recent philosophers have laboured
to reconcile Plato with Aristotle; but John deems the attempt
futile. It is clear that they differed. Another group of Realists
holds that universals are natural forms, images of the divine Ideas
dwelling in created things. Others assert that universality consists
in the combination of particulars; while others propound the
doctrine of *maneries*, the meaning of which John is unable to
interpret.[1]

Thus, soon after the death of Abaelard, all the opinions discussed
by him were still being warmly debated. It must be added that
John himself in a careful discussion of the question, closely faithful
to Aristotle, arrives at conclusions similar to those of his master.
The mind has the power of abstracting and recombining common
aspects of particulars. Anyone who seeks to grasp these abstractions apart from the particulars is searching for dreams. A man
would not thank you for the gift of a horse-in-general. Universals
are ways of apprehending and of thinking of particulars, ways
which are necessary to our minds; they are not objects in their own
right.[2]

Abaelard's place in the history of Scholasticism lies in his
analytical method. The distinctive characteristic of his manner of
philosophizing is his persistent criticisms of the meaning of words.

---

[1] The word appears to be derived from *mannaria*, meaning 'way of handling' or
'manner'. C. C. J. Webb, *Metalogicon*, p. 95, note.
[2] Cf. op. cit. ii. 20.

Later sections of the treatises we have been describing contain many examples of this method. There are acute examinations of the meaning of the words 'and', 'all', 'anyone', and 'someone'. And there is an elaborate treatment of the import of propositions. Logical conceptions, he is always insisting, must not be taken as referring naïvely to things. Words and sentences express various arbitrary senses given to things. Philosophy is the science of the meanings which words express. The theory of knowledge must be preceded by a critical discussion of language. This method founded a school of logicians who based their science upon an investigation into the meaning of grammatical forms. 'Grammar is the cradle of all philosophy', wrote John of Salisbury. The names of representatives of this school, Lambert of Auxerre, Peter of Spain, William of Shyreswood, indicate the range of this movement. Through these philosophers the method passed to William of Ockham whose Nominalism developed the conceptual elements in Abaelard, with disturbing results for Scholastic thought.

F

ST. THOMAS AQUINAS

REFERENCES

All references to the *Summa Theologica* are to the Questions and Articles of the First Part. Other references are to the *Summa contra Gentiles, De Ente et Essentia, De Potentiis Animae, Quaestiones Disputatae de Veritate, IV libri Sententiarum,* and *De Anima.*

I

DURING the thirteenth century the philosophical thought of Europe was transformed. The chief factor in this new development was the rediscovery of some of the cardinal works of ancient reflection. From the middle of the twelfth century in Sicily and in the Spanish peninsula numerous translators were engaged in producing Latin versions from the Arabic records of Greek science and philosophy. A generation earlier Abaelard, as we have seen, was acquainted with but a few of the minor logical works of Aristotle. Now not only the major logical treatises but the *Physics* and the *Metaphysics* were for the first time made available for study. The impact was disturbing, for it was revealed that on many vital points of Christian thought Aristotle's views were at variance with the teaching of the Church. The disparity was exaggerated by the way in which the philosopher's thought was interpreted by Avicenna and Averroës, the great Arab scholars through whom Aristotle's writings were first transmitted to Christian students. Aristotle was presented as maintaining views on providence, on the eternity of the world, on the reality of individuals, on freedom, and on immortality, which were in direct contradiction with Christian beliefs. Repeatedly throughout the thirteenth century masters were forbidden to instruct their students in the doctrines of the philosopher who was soon to become the standard authority of medieval reflection. Conservative theologians recoiled from these dangerous innovations and reasserted the claims of Augustinianism and of Neoplatonism. Others interpreted Aristotle in Augustinian terms.

In order to appreciate the work achieved by Thomas Aquinas it is essential to realize that his independent analysis of thought and reality led him into conflict with both the influential schools of philosophy which were actively disputing at his side. He was compelled to criticize the Neoplatonism of Bonaventura on the one hand, the Arabian conception of Aristotle on the other. The latter position was being powerfully advocated by Siger of Brabant and other contemporary philosophers. It is true that a comprehensive exploration into the implications of Aristotle had been made by Thomas's master, Albert the Great (1206–80). It was he who attempted for the first time the task of reconciling Aristotle with Christian doctrine. He addressed himself to the formidable labour of paraphrasing and commenting upon the entire range of treatises of the Stagirite. In carrying through this colossal work Albert performed an inestimable service to medieval thought. Unfortunately he was content to describe many theories which in default of more precise interpretation appeared to be inconsistent with one another; and to this eclecticism is added a diffuseness which constantly leads the reader from the point at issue.

But the immense labour by which the mass of new material was examined and incorporated into Christian thought was accomplished by Thomas of Aquino. Early in his career he encouraged the distinguished scholar, William of Moerbeke, to undertake a series of translations from the authentic text of Aristotle. And his own numerous commentaries on the treatises of the philosopher sought to expound the genuine meaning of the conceptions found in them. What Thomas perceived in this philosophy, freed from Arabic and from Augustinian interpretation, was a systematic doctrine of knowledge and reality that fulfilled the demands of experience and of human nature. The constant endeavour of his doctrine of knowledge is directed to bringing together into one pattern of experience both the universal, immaterial elements, and the particular, material features of thought. Such a programme means, in the sphere of mental processes, the work of harmonizing the claims of sensation and conception; in relation to objects it means the due recognition of both contingent material entities and necessary universal 'ideas'. In the Aristotelian theory he found justice done to both sides of experience.

Thomas's father was the Count of Aquino and he was born at the castle of Roccasicca near Naples in 1225. He received his early education at the local Benedictine Abbey of Monte Cassino, leaving there at the age of fourteen to continue his studies at the University of Naples which had lately been founded by the Emperor Frederick II. At the age of twenty Thomas decided to enter the teaching order of the Dominicans, and was sent by his superiors to Paris in order to pursue higher studies in theology.

His decision to become a friar annoyed his family, and he was seized on his journey by his two brothers and held captive in the castle of St. Giovanni. Here he was detained for a year. All efforts to persuade him to abandon the religious life for one more appropriate to his noble station proved unavailing, and he was at length allowed to continue his journey to Paris. There he came under the immediate influence of Albert of Cologne. Much has been written on the relation of Thomas's thought to the work of Albert the Great. The debt of the disciple has been exaggerated; but Thomas's reflections certainly owed much to the vast scholarship of Albert. Thomas accompanied his master to Cologne in 1248, where Albert had been charged with the task of establishing a school of higher studies. On his return to Paris four years later he entered on his course for the degree of Master of Theology. He attained his licence for teaching in 1256. A letter from the Pope Alexander IV has been preserved in which he expresses his pleasure to the Chancellor of the University 'in having granted the licence for teaching in the faculty of theology to our beloved son friar Thomas of Aquino of the Order of Preachers, a man of noble birth and renowned for the regularity of his life and by the grace of God learned in the whole range of letters'. Thomas had already published several works which gave promise of the strength of his mind.

A short period of teaching at the University was followed by a recall to Italy where he composed his *Summa Contra Gentiles*. During nine years he taught theology in his native country, chiefly at the papal court. Already he had attained a position of high distinction as a philosopher, and he was also called upon to perform many tasks in educational administration. In 1268 he was appointed to lecture on Theology at the University of Paris, where he found himself plunged in controversy with the leaders of the secular clergy on the one hand and with the followers of the traditional method of Aristotelianism, whose spokesman was Siger of Brabant. The Averroistic interpretation of Aristotle was finally condemned by the Bishop of Paris in 1270, principally owing to Thomas's incisive exposure of its fallacies. But at the height of his fame he was in 1272 once more recalled to Italy, where he was entrusted with the direction of the theological curriculum for the Dominican Order in that country. He worked for two years in Naples. In 1274 he was invited by Pope Gregory X to take part in the Council of Lyons which had been summoned to discuss the unity of the Church. On the journey he fell ill, and at the Cistercian monastery of Fossanuova near Terracina he died on 7 March 1274 at the early age of forty-eight.

Thomas produced an astonishing amount of works ranging throughout the compass of philosophy and theology. He wrote twelve books of commentaries on Aristotle, twenty philosophical treatises, and a large number of works on theology, on the religious life, and on exegesis. His two most celebrated works are the *Summa Contra Gentiles*, which he composed for the benefit of Catholic missionaries among the heathen, and the vast *Summa Theologica*. In this work, which comprises three parts, thirty-eight treatises, 631 questions, and about 3,000 articles, the entire range of theology and philosophy is surveyed, the nature of God, the life of the angels, and that world of mingled intelligence and matter, the human mind.

The rigorous style of the philosopher affords few glimpses of the man. From his biographers we receive a picture of a saintly scholar with extraordinary powers of application. His day was so filled with prayer, composition, and teaching that he had little time for food and sleep. He was always engrossed in reflection and it was found necessary to appoint a companion to guide him in the practical necessities of life. His intellectual concentration was so remarkable that he was able to dictate to several secretaries at the same time. Thomas's writings display an almost Euclidean clarity and rigour. The question at issue is first stated. This is followed by a series of difficulties or objections to the position stated. Next, arguments or pronouncements expressing a contrary view are given. Now follows the main body of the article, in which the position advocated by the author is set forth. Finally the objections proposed at the beginning are criticized or explained in the light of the principles expounded in the main section of the article. An example of this method, the finest development of Scholastic procedure, is given on a later page.

II

St. Thomas's language concerning the relation of mind to the world it apprehends seems at first sight to embrace contrary positions. On the one hand we are told that the mind grasps immediately, without representative interference, the objects which confront it. The objects of knowledge differ radically from mental processes. That which is primarily known is not composed of states of consciousness, whether impressions or ideas or the self.

For human understanding the first object of knowledge is 'aliquid extrinsecum, scilicet natura materialis rei', something external, the nature of a material thing. The operations by which the subject is known is a secondary and indirect type of knowledge, *secundario cognoscitur ipse actus*.[1]

On the other hand, Thomas's assertions frequently appear to deny this position. We find him saying that the first thing understood by the intellect is its own act of understanding. The world of which the mind is aware is described in terms that seem to mean that it is infected with subjective elements. Material things so far as they are known must exist in the knower, not indeed materially, but immaterially. The intellect in act is the object understood in act. The realm of objects is a mode of the same reality which is found in consciousness; there is an essential kinship, a correspondence, between mind and things. In its relation to mind being must first correspond to the intellect. Things are ideas.[2]

The business of knowing is therefore both a direct approach to objects external to the mind, and also the expression of what is in some way already in the mind. 'All knowledge is through some form which is the principle of knowledge in the knower.' But, 'it is the stone which is understood not the likeness of the stone'.[3]

The resolution of these apparent contradictions naturally follows upon an interpretation of Thomas's terms; and the attempt to explain them must take us to the heart not merely of his doctrine of knowledge but also of his conception of reality. His accounts of perception and of thought will be totally misconceived if they are detached from his philosophy of being. A summary description of the cardinal principles of his metaphysics must, however inadequately, be attempted.

These principles are Aristotelian. Fundamentally, Reality is absolute and unchanging. But the Real is conceived of as an End, and every aspect of the Universe is teleological. All that exists and all that happens exists and happens for the sake of some outcome, near or remote. The ultimate explanation of individual things and events lies in the end which they subserve. For our experience things are pervaded by change.[4] And no change is meaningless; it is, on the one hand, relative to some stage or culmination,

---

[1] Q. lxxxv. 2, lxxxvii. 3.

[2] Q. lxxxvii. 3, lxxxiv. 2, lxxxvii. 1.   [3] Q. lxxvi. 2 and 4.

[4] As we shall notice later forms are not subject to change. They are always actual.

on the other hand, it implies preparation. It is a becoming. But becoming presupposes something which does not become, an attainment and state of rest. Accordingly there is implicated in every type of existence and event a twofold condition. These two aspects of being are expressed by the terms *actus* and *potentia* which represent Aristotle's ἐνέργεια and δύναμις. The conception of act and potency animates every department of Thomas's thought. All modes of being, a stone, an oak-tree, a man, are conceived of as realizations. Every form of activity and change, all growth and decay, are to be understood in relation to ends or fulfilments. They are tendencies. At any stage of its existence a thing whether animate or inanimate, whether a rock or a dog, is in respect to another stage in potency. For any entity that is undergoing change is not complete. It is approaching a determination of its nature, or it is receding from it. And this determination *is* its real nature. In so far as a thing has achieved stability or perfection it is *in actu*. In so far as it shows aptitude for a more enduring and determinate state of existence it is *in potentia*. A thing is indeterminate the more it expresses its nature independently of other things. In a word, the more immanent the process which sustains the thing the more it possesses of reality. The further it is self-determined the higher it is in the scale of being.

It is important to notice that neither act nor potency can occur independently of one another. Potency presupposes act. It is only through the actual that what is potential can exist. All learning, to adopt an example of St. Thomas's, comes from knowledge that exists already, not only in the teacher but also in the learner. On the other hand if potency disappeared there would be no movement, process, activity. But the process is not independent of the outcome. Entities are not produced by it. There *is* something, an identity, which changes. Modern principles such as an *élan vital* or a space-time which creates orders different from themselves would be, on this view, abstractions. For all processes are actuated by ends which are already implicit in them.[1] Change of any kind is the invasion of a potency by an act. Acts are in fact ideals to which any activity approximates, and the ideal governs and pervades each stage of the activity. Thomas thus avoids on the one hand a naturalism which tries to account for the higher levels of experience in terms of the lower; while he escapes on the other side an all-engulfing absolute for which every process is an appearance,

[1] Q. lxxxiii. 3 ad 2.

a pseudo-reality. For if the whole is ultimately in act, nothing can become. But potency is not an illusion. It is a constant aspect of the real finite world. Beyond this world, indeed, Faith points to an infinite Reality, a Being to whom no change can be attributed; for what is absolutely real cannot cease to be itself.

The numerous further distinctions which Thomas elaborates within Being, substance and accident, being and essence, essence and existence, effect and end, analogy and causality, the doctrine of degrees of perfection, must all be understood in the light of this fundamental rhythm. Its applications are indeed infinite. All the categories evince this twofold character. But for the theory of knowledge the dominating application is that of Matter and Form.[1] Matter is the underlying amorphous element of which things are made. It is pure passive potency and requires form for its actual expression. Form is the realization of matter in definite structures or patterns. Matter is constantly being transformed by an inherent activity into determinate shapes. The nebulous substratum, ὕλη, becomes substances in virtue of form. We have notices that the process and direction of potency is governed by act. So the movement immanent in matter is due to form. *Omnis actio est per formam.* Form is the principle of completion and accordingly it is the essential principle of everything's existence. 'The substantial form makes a thing to exist absolutely.'[2] Health is determined by a form of health; heat by a form of heat. Above all, as we shall see, mind is the form of the body. But the form of anything is not to be conceived as an entity or nucleus alongside the material element. It is the organizing principle of the material element, that which makes it a unity, or a thing.

Form, in fact, gives existence to matter, for matter cannot exist without some structure. But form is not dependent on matter. Thomas believed that intellectual beings can, in principle, exist without material embodiment. But such beings would be simple substances. Human beings are composite substances and their essences embrace form and matter.[3]

In all this what is potency and matter, what is act and form, are points of relative emphasis. In different references what is potency may become act and what is act may be seen to be potency. The

---

[1] Some authorities regard Potency and Act as themselves derived from Matter and Form. See Sertillanges, *Saint Thomas d'Aquin*, Paris, 1910, ii, p. 8.

[2] Q. lxxvii. 6. Thomas distinguishes substances of various kinds from accidental forms. The former are natural, the latter are artificial and man-made.

[3] *De Ente et Essentia*, 4.

stones of a house are potency in relation to the house, but the stones may be viewed as themselves acts for they are the consummation of processes which have gone to make them. In bare matter these correlative principles are expressed in the distinction between the elements into which anything can be analysed and the thing itself as a unity. It is one in virtue of a Form, it is many in virtue of its matter. In the field of living creatures it is due to their materiality that they are many individuals.[1]

It is in the organic realm that the application of these principles is most clear. The growth of a blade of grass or a horse or a man is intelligible only in relation to the maturity of these types of being. Growth in organisms points throughout to a culminating stage in which the structural plan found in detail throughout the organism discovers its completion. The principle still further illuminates ethical and aesthetic experience. It throws light on the teleological character of goodness. The nature of a person, and indeed the nature of any activity judged good, is directed to a certain fulfilment. Goodness is the domination of an activity by an immanent form which is also its end. Not that a person makes his own goodness. For St. Thomas goodness is ultimately communicated.[2]

This central principle is further developed in another celebrated and difficult Thomistic doctrine, that of essence and existence. In the content of my awareness of anything, this inkpot or this dog, I can distinguish in theory two elements. I am aware that it is an inkpot and I am aware that it exists. In the former aspect I apprehend the object as possessing a characteristic shape and a particular purpose, and by these I am able to define it and to distinguish it from other objects. The essence is what an object is. It is the source of all its properties. Essences are universals. The essence or nature of an object includes only those elements which fall under the definition of species, just as humanity or man in general includes those features which fall under the definition of man. In virtue of these features man *is* man ; humanity means that by which man is man.[3] But we can conceive such essences without assuming that they actually exist. Actual existence implies a further principle. To the unity of the inkpot, dog, or man is added

---

[1] It must be admitted that there seems to be incompatibility between the conception of matter as the unconditioned manifold and the principle, equally cardinal in Thomas, that matter is the foundation of individuality.

[2] On the application of *actus* and *potentia* to goodness see A. E. Taylor, *Aristotelian Society*, Supplementary Vol., xi, p. 158.

[3] Q. iii. 3.

the contingent multiple shapes by which these natures are actually expressed. It does not follow that essences have any form of being, or subsist, apart from existence. What the principle does assert is that existence is not necessary to essence. Thomas believed in and describes at length an order of beings, the angels, whose natures approach a unity of essence and existence.[1] The essence of an angel is fully expressed in himself. Yet even here the two principles fall apart. An angel does not derive his existence from his essence. He does not create himself. The existence of a thing cannot be caused by the essence of the thing. If this were so the thing would bring itself into existence. Everything which exists derives its existence from something else. If we press this derivation back far enough we arrive at an ultimate cause of all things, a being which essentially exists.[2]

We have here another facet of the idea of act and potency. Essences are potencies to the act of existence. But no creatures attain fully to their potency; all contingent existences fall short of their capabilities.

III

St. Thomas's theory of knowledge must be understood according to the general conceptions of which we have given an outline. The passage from ignorance to knowledge is an aspect of the universal rhythm of potency and act. And it is a specialized expression of the determination of matter by form. It displays a mode of the growth of an organism to maturity. Knowing is a manner of being, a maturing of the immanent life of mind. In the process of understanding from simple apprehension to philosophical reflection the mind seeks the perfection of its own nature. Cognition is the peculiar achievement of life at the level of mind. A new synthesis of being is here reached. Mind or intentional being transcends life and physical existence, natural being. The activities of the vegetable and animal world are concerned with their immediate environment. The life of mind is aware of wider reaches of time and space; and it is conscious of its own awareness. But the distinctive mark of mental activity is that it does not effect any alteration in the objects with which it unites. Inferior orders of life, plants and lowly animal organisms, 'know' their environment by assimilating it or by other action upon it. Mind feeds on the world without altering it. Objects do not enter in any bodily form into mind, nor does mind contribute anything to the nature of objects. An object is

[1] Q. lii ff.   [2] De Ente et Essentia, 4.

external and yet it is known as a mode of mental being. In the object the form has a natural being, *esse naturale*, in the mind it has a mental being, *esse spirituale* or *intentionale*.

On a rationalist metaphysic Thomas thus imposes an empiricist theory of knowledge, in the modern senses of these terms. In a celebrated passage he states the position thus. The ancient naturalists, of whom Democritus was typical, saw that object and subject must have something in common, but they concluded that this common principle was identical in nature with either mind or matter. These naturalists resolved the dualism by materializing mind. Plato, on the other hand, resolved it by idealizing objects. He observed that mind is immaterial and believed that the things which it knows subsist as immaterial forms. Thomas replies to the materialists, firstly, that the process of knowing is not the production of physical objects; secondly, that if the material objects exist in their material form in the knower, one might as well say that anything knows. 'If by fire the mind knows fire, fire itself would be conscious of itself. But things which only receive forms materially are determined to a particular thing; the form does not extend to other things. Now the characteristic of knowing is that it refers to a number of things outside the particular knower.'[1] On the one hand, then, the primary object of knowledge is in no way a psychic entity; it is material. Yet, on the other, there is an identity of subject and object which is fundamental to experience. The mind in exploring the external world expresses itself. 'Cognoscens in actu est cognitum in actu.' The problem of knowledge is to explain this transference; to show how mind without ceasing to be itself becomes something strangely different. And on the other hand, the external object of which mind is aware must be shown to unite with mind without modification of its own nature.

There are two modes by which things can influence or act upon one another. All transformations, as we have seen, take place under the influence of a form. We have now to notice that the form may be transferred in two ways. It may be physically transferred from one body to another. When, for example, a piece of bread is heated the heat in the fire passes into the bread. This type of action is termed natural change, *immutatio naturalis*. 'Natural alteration takes place when the form of that which alters is received into that which is altered in its actual state as heat passes into what is heated.'[2]

[1] Q. lxxxiv. 2.   [2] Q. lxxviii. 3, cf. 2.

Now in sense-perception some natural change occurs. The physical change may occur in the object. In order to produce sound the object must be struck; in order to produce smell 'a body must to· some degree be affected by heat'. But the change occurs also in the physical organ. 'The hand that touches something hot becomes hot, while the tongue is moistened by the humidity of the flavoured morsel.'[1] But there is another mode of the alteration of one object by another. This is mental change, *immutatio spiritualis*. Here the form of the object is received into the thing which is changed by it 'according to a spiritual mode of existence'. What receives the form does not do so in any physical manner. Materially it is unaffected by the change. The operation of knowledge is of this kind. The form of colour received into the pupil of the eye does not change the colour of the eye. In Thomas's language an *intentio* of the sensible form is affected in the sensory organ. By *intentio* is meant an apprehension of something.

The forms of objects are incarnate; they are expressed in matter. The mind cannot attain the materialized forms of objects. It reaches out to and assimilates the forms only in so far as they are communicable. And what renders them communicable are *similitudines*, likenesses of objects. But consciousness of objects does not lie in the mere possession of a likeness by the mind. It consists in the degree according to which the likeness represents the object. But we must defer for the moment further discussion of the status of *similitudo*.

Knowledge, then, takes place in virtue of an assimilation of the knower to the object known.[2] 'The more anything is known, the more intimate is the understanding of it, the more is it one with the knower.' Mind and its objects are thus linked by an essential kinship. Knowledge is due to the presence and effects of the object; object is different from the subject; but it is also a phase of the self-actualization of the subject. The mind in the course of perfecting itself seeks to know objects.

We are perhaps now in a position to grasp the paradoxical phrases quoted earlier. Knowledge is concerned immediately with objects, but also with what is already in the mind. For reality is expressed not only in matter but also under certain conditions in a conscious subject. The chief of these conditions is the immateriality of the subject. For the object, as we have seen, penetrates the subject by means of an ideal form of which it is the material

[1] Q. lxxviii. 3. [2] De Ver. i. 1.

embodiment. Its material configuration is controlled by a form so as to be what it is, a stone, a fire, or a work of art. On the other hand, the mind in knowing passes beyond itself without ceasing to be itself. The ideal form in the subject unites with the forms of the external world. This is the meaning of Thomas's oft-repeated assertions that the form of that which is known is in the knower, and that understanding in act is the object understood in act.

But in order to study more precisely the bearing of these principles upon perception and thought we must turn to St. Thomas's view of the relation between body and mind.

IV

We have noticed that for St. Augustine and for the dominant tradition of medieval thought which followed him the mind is a nature wholly different from the body. The body belongs to the physical realm. It is, in the main, passive to external influences of a material type, and has no influence on the mind. The mind is active and produces sensations from its own substance.

St. Thomas begins by asserting no less the incorporeal nature of mind. Mind is *intellectus* or understanding and understanding is immaterial and subsistent. Mind is not composed of matter and form. In principle *intellectus* knows a thing absolutely. It knows the form of a stone, that is to say it knows it as substance in general. If it apprehended the stone as matter it would apprehend it through a bodily organ and therefore as an individual object. Further St. Thomas maintains that the understanding as such is immune from decay. It is not liable to change because it is not an existent; it is a subsistent form. The senses do not know existence save under conditions of *here* and *now*, whereas the understanding knows things absolutely and eternally. So far, Thomas adheres completely to St. Augustine's way of thought.[1]

But the great difference between that philosophy and his own is that he does not think that the mind as such, pure understanding, functions in our experience. The mind of man is not a pure intelligence (such as an angel) nor is it a spirit in a corpse. It is an organic composite of mind and body. For human beings mind is the form of the body. The cause of activity is a form of the thing which is active. For example, the fundamental cause of healing is the form of health, and the fundamental cause of the mind's

[1] Q. lxxv. 5, 6.

knowledge is the form of knowledge. Now mind is manifested at all levels of nature, and at the lower levels it appears as life. Life shows itself according to different operations in different degrees of living things; but the principle of all vital functions, whether nourishment or sensation or movement, is the mind. Mind is the organic principle; it cannot be severed from the organism without ceasing to be itself. Thus when St. Thomas says that the mind is the form of the body he means that it determines the character of the body. A human body could not be a body apart from mind; and a mind divided from its body ceases to be a mind.[1]

Mind, in fact, virtually contains the sensitive and nutritive functions and all inferior forms.[2] Looked at as functions these inferior forms *are* mind. We must not suppose, however, that the human mind is composed of several distinct forms. The doctrine of the plurality of forms, warmly defended in the thirteenth century, is rejected. The organic mind, the perceptive mind, and the understanding constitute one mind. And this mind pervades the whole body.[3] Mind cannot function at the level of sensation without material expression; for the process of sensing is accompanied by changes in the body. The act of seeing is accompanied by changes in the eye, and so with the other senses. Every operation of the sensory mind is an operation of the joint activity of body-mind.[4] And man's knowledge is rooted in sensation. Without this reference to particulars man's knowledge would be imperfect, of a general nature and confused. It is therefore with a view to having perfect and proper knowledge of things that human minds are constituted by nature to be united to bodies, and thus to receive the proper and adequate knowledge of sensible things from the actual things; they are like uneducated persons who cannot be instructed without concrete examples. It is clear, then, that the greater good of the mind requires its union with the body and that it understands by relying on sensible images.[5] But the understanding knows corporeal objects by a knowledge which is immaterial. In so far, then, as human knowledge can attain understanding it transcends the body.

The position is approached in one passage in the following way. Anyone who examines his consciousness is aware that it is one and the same self who experiences both thinking and sensation. But sensation requires a body; therefore the body must be a part of self.[6]

[1] Q. lxxxix. 1.   [2] Q. lxxvi. 4.   [3] Q. iii. 8.
[4] Q. lxxvi. 3.   [5] Q. lxxxix. 1.   [6] Q. lxxvi. 1.

Body and mind form one complex being, man. His mind is not disembodied; it is not a soul in a machine. The unity which Thomas seeks to explain is an intimate one. The mind is not related to the body as an agent to his instrument nor as a pilot to his ship, as Plato maintained. The assumption here is that the essential nature of man lies in his mind; his body is as external to him as his clothes. But the body and its organs form part of the essence of man, for the mind is expressed in sensation as well as in thought.[1]

One consequence of this union is that minds are individualized; for the bodies of which they are parts are, as matter, necessarily particular. All men do not constitute one mind, as certain types of extreme Realism had held. St. Thomas points out, in the manner of Abaelard, that if this position were true it would follow that two men would be essentially one, differing only in accidents. Socrates and Plato would differ in no other respect than one man with a shirt differs from another with a cloak. And this, Thomas observes, is quite absurd.[2]

Since, then, the human mind is intimately allied with matter its thinking is throughout infected with sensible experience. This interpretation of the roots of human knowledge is a striking departure from the traditional position, which, as we have noticed, was still being asserted and developed by St. Bonaventura and the Franciscans. The central thesis that the mind knows material objects in the 'eternal reasons' is directly examined. Thomas begins by quoting a text from St. Augustine's *Confessions* in which the objectivity of truth is maintained. 'If we both see that what you say is true and if we both see that what I say is true, where do we see this, pray? I do not see it in you, nor do you see it in me; but we both see it in the unchangeable truth which is above our minds.'[3] The unchangeable truth lies in the eternal Ideas, and in them all reality, including the reality of material objects, is known. In his reply to this position Thomas first points out the difference between the formulation of the Platonic doctrine by Augustine and Plato's own expression of it. Plato had held that the Forms of things subsist apart from matter. These Forms are conceived of as creative substances, the source of a thing's existence. Such a view is inadmissible in the Christian Faith for which God alone is the source of all being. For this reason Augustine set the Ideas in the divine mind.

Thomas now directly considers the Realist position by inquiring

[1] *De Anima* Q. i. i.　　　[2] Q. lxxvi. 2.　　　[3] Confess. XII. xxv. 35.

what is meant by a thing being known in something. There are two senses in which this statement can be taken. Firstly it can be taken literally. An object can be known, or apprehended, in another object which is itself already known, as for example in a mirror. Now under the conditions of human life the mind cannot see things in the eternal reasons in this sense, that is to say, as reflections of the divine mind. This is only possible to spiritual beings, who see God. But secondly, a thing can be apprehended in something in the sense of being known by means of something. Thus we might say that we see in the sun what we see by means of the sun. In this sense we can say that the human mind knows all things in the eternal reasons since all intelligent experience is ultimately derived from God; our light of reason bears some likeness to the uncreated Light. But the vital consideration is that the intelligible content of experience is for us derived from things, not from eternal reasons. Thomas happily quotes a passage from Augustine himself in which the importance of perceptual experience is pointed out.[1] 'Although the philosophers prove by convincing arguments that all things occur in time according to the eternal reasons, were they able to see in the eternal reasons or to find out from them how many kinds of animals there are and the origin of each? Did not they seek this information from the story of times and places?' Our knowledge is dependent upon sensory experience.[2]

Again he rejects the Platonic belief that the mind contains innate ideas through which it has knowledge independently of experience. The argument of the *Meno* is recalled, where Plato seeks to prove that we have *a priori* knowledge. In the course of that dialogue a person of no education gives true answers to a series of questions in geometry. In considering this point Thomas relies on the principles of potency and act. Mind apart from experience is in potency; its thought is only in act when instruction or experience is brought to bear on the potential state. Plato had maintained that the mind has the capacity of attaining knowledge of universals but is hindered by its connexion with the body and with sensation. But if the mind possesses by nature this universal knowledge it is difficult to understand why it should forget it. The root of the Platonic belief is a denial of the natural unity of body and mind. If mind is by nature united with the body it is unreasonable to maintain that it is hindered by the body. Knowledge of the type insisted on by the Platonists, knowledge of universals divorced

[1] De Trin. iv. 16.   [2] Q. lxxxiv. a 5.

from sensory reference, could not include apprehension of material objects. For this apprehension requires sensory experience. A man born blind has no knowledge of colour. As for the argument of the *Meno*, universal self-evident principles are not known previously to being elicitated. Then they are known for the first time. Once seen their consequence can be also seen under systematic questioning.[1]

Human knowledge is dependent upon perceptual experience. Our minds cannot free themselves of sensory references even in reflection upon 'the eternal truths'. Even in these regions we do not attain a mode of knowledge which shares in an order of perfectly intelligible and certain ideas, devoid of all the contingency of sense. Incorporeal principles are known to us only through sensible bodies. The human mind holds a middle place between organic beings whose information extends no further than the environment with which they are in immediate contact, and the angels who are able to know material objects not through the senses, but in the immaterial principles. In our present state we cannot understand separate immaterial substances in themselves. If our intellectual power were capable of acting apart from sense it could not be obstructed by damage to a sensory organ. But we find that such damage, as in epilepsy, makes a man unable to use his mind.[2]

V

The human mind exhibits a number of capacities or potencies because it lies in the order of being between the spiritual and physical realms and the activities proper to each meet together in it. But it is not therefore resoluble into a number of separated functions. For the various activities which enter into knowing are potencies; they are tendencies which seek fulfilment. Mind is in essence act; and this means that it is a unity in which activities are completed, and to which they are subordinate.[3]

The broad division of powers is between the sensitive and intellectual. The former is effected by the particular. Its seat is the composite body-mind, where various activities consequent upon the stimulus of a sense-organ combine to form the elementary perception of the external world. The seat of the intellectual power, the processes of thought and reason, is that part of the mind which surpasses matter. Its object is the essence of particular things.

[1] Q. lxxxiv. 3.   [2] Q. lxxxiv. 7.   [3] Q. lxxvii. 2.

G

In describing the psychological elements which enter into perception Thomas, following Aristotle, adopts a biological approach. These processes are the outcome of activities which are manifested at humbler levels of life. The activities of living bodies are distinguished in general from the movements of wholly material bodies by the fact that they are directed from without. The various levels of life and mind are accordingly marked off from one another by the scope of the field of reality to which they are capable of referring. At a lowly level the creature is concerned with no more than the fundamental functions of its body, the rhythms of generation, growth, and nutrition. This is the vegetative level of existence, characteristic of plants. What knowledge they possess extends no further than what is immediately present to them. It is expressed in movements which respond to actual stimulus. Knowledge proper begins at a further stage. For the sensitive or perceptual order of life there is awareness of a world existing independently of the creature. But this experience is intrinsically united with appetite and instinct, and it becomes more explicit with increasing range of movement.[1]

The psychology of this perceptual and animal level of mind, in which the mind of man is rooted, is elaborated, with some modifications, upon the Aristotelian model of which Thomas is able to make better use than his predecessors. Perception requires not only the five outer senses, but also a number of inner senses. Among these Thomas distinguishes firstly a *sensus communis* or general sensibility. All experience presupposes the unity of organic life, an enduring and pervasive centre of awareness from which the special senses are derived and to which they refer. To this organic sensibility are assigned several types of experience. Not only does it co-ordinate the deliverances of the separate senses; by it the mind is enabled to be aware that it is conscious.[2] Self-consciousness grows from this root. Further, *sensus communis* distinguishes between the experiences of the different senses.[3] The simultaneous perception of two qualities such as hard and sweet implies a common sensibility. Lastly an important function must be mentioned. This sense perceives the common sensibles, such qualities in things, that is to say, as movement, rest, size, shape, number. These properties are not apprehended by any particular sense, as are the sense qualities, odour, sound, colour, yet they are sensory qualities.[4]

[1] Q. lxxviii. 1, 2.   [2] Q. lxxviii. 4.   [3] Q. i. 3 ad 2.   [4] De Pot. An. iv.

In the animal mind Thomas finds a capacity which he names *vis aestimativa*. It corresponds closely to the modern conception of instinct. In placing it at the basis of primitive apprehension Thomas rejects hedonist theories of action. An animal is not moved to avoid or to desire the objects before it only because they are felt to be pleasing or not pleasing, but also on account of other benefits and uses, or disadvantages. Thus a sheep runs away when it sees a wolf, not on account of the ugliness of the creature's colour or shape, but because it is a natural enemy. And in the same way a bird gathers together straw, not because it gives pleasure to its senses, but because the straw is useful for building its nest. An animal, therefore, must recognize ideas (*intentiones*) of this kind, though its external senses do not apprehend their significance.[1] Animals, in fact, are predisposed to attend to certain sensory patterns; their behaviour cannot be accounted for on the basis of associations derived from experience, still less on the score of unrelated presentations. In man the ideas which are implicit in instinct become explicit by the exercise of a kind of comparison (*per quandam collationem*). In *De Potentiis Animae*[2] Thomas makes a suggestive comparison between this instinctive capacity in animals and man's intellectual life. Just as the animal through its *vis aestimativa* is aware of more than what is given to it in sensation, so man knows more than what his senses reveal, even though his knowledge arises from sense.

The awareness of sensory images, *phantasmata*, is placed among the interior senses. But *phantasia* or *imaginatio* includes also, somewhat confusingly, the power of retaining impressions, and this form of retention is distinguished from memory, *vis memorativa*, which is devoted to the preservation of ideas. In man this power develops into recall, *reminiscentia*, the active effort to form associations.

Now that the psychological processes which may be discerned at the perceptual level of life have been sketched, we may appropriately raise the philosophical issue concerning the validity of these activities. Knowledge, we have seen, begins with mental sensations which are the counterpart of physical impressions. We must bear in mind the immanent character of the activity implied in this description. Sensible knowledge unfolds in response to a physical alteration of the sense-organ, but the process is fundamentally a movement of the form which exists in different modes in mind and

[1] Q. lxxviii. 4. [2] Op. cit. iv.

in thing. Sensation is to the sense-organ what mind is to body. Sensation is the realization, the act, of the sense-organ.

The mental sensory elements are *phantasmata*, and our thought is dependent upon them. But they do not comprise the only content of perception. For their objects are particular and private, while the objects we perceive are universal and public. When I perceive a stone I receive a multitude of different images, and another man has a series of images which differ from mine. Yet I perceive one stone and I and my friend perceive the same stone. What is apprehended is not a pattern of evanescent images but an object. And this must be, at least, a unity having diverse aspects.[1] In a word it must be a universal, and this, we shall see, is the only element which mind can directly apprehend.

Images are not objects, but they are necessary to the experience of objects. Their function is to provoke consciousness and to orientate thought. Sensorial impressions free the intelligible. They are signs. Mind responds to the stimulus of the *phantasmata* in the sense of using them in the production of the generalized form which is the object of consciousness. The form implicated in matter is unknowable. Only in so far as it is extracted, that is to say becomes universal, can it be apprehended.[2]

It follows that *phantasmata* are not directly known. Our minds know only the universal directly. But the particular element in experience can be known indirectly, by a kind of reflection. We can attend to images as elements in our experience by isolating them artificially. The sensible images as such can only enter into consciousness when they are stripped of sensibility. If we try to take them as representations we must be careful to say that they represent no more than subjective contacts with objects, not the objects as they are. These references show the remarkable advance made by Thomas on the psychology of his predecessors. There is a nice recognition of both the universal and particular ingredients of experience.

Augustine's observation that *phantasmata* taken by themselves (so far as they can be so taken) are only able to report the pictures they present, and that these are subjectively true, is quoted with approval.[3] It is only when they are referred to objects that the question of their truth or falsity arises. For instance when we see a white object through green glass we question the validity of the appearance. 'The understanding judges of the pretensions offered

[1] Q. lxxvi. 2.   [2] Contra Gent. 1. 44; cf. ib. iii. 84.   [3] Q. Disp. i, De Ver. 11.

by the senses.' If sensations were the only components of knowledge every sensation would be true, even contradictory ones.
There would be no means of distinguishing reality from illusion.[1]

The cardinal error is the separation of two modes of knowledge,
perception and thought. Two extreme positions have been held,
each determined by exclusive interest in one aspect of experience.
For two orders are discovered in reflection, one the order of
unchanging and necessary entities such as logical and mathematical principles, the other the realm of changing and contingent
things, material objects and the bodies of creatures. These are
perceived by the senses, the former are known by the understanding. Augustine, we have seen, had denied that bodies could be
known by the understanding. Intellect and sense are distinct and
have different spheres. Understanding cannot know bodies, nor
sense essences or forms.

Thomas points out that if sense is divided from thought knowledge becomes impossible. If we suppose, with Heracleitus, that
there is nothing in experience but what is apprehended by the
senses, experience becomes a perpetual flux. And what is in a state
of continual flux cannot be an object of knowledge; for *this* state
ceases to be and is replaced by another before the mind can say
what it is. If on the other hand we hold, with Plato, that over
and above material things there is a realm of eternal Ideas, from
which particular existences draw their being, other difficulties arise.
In the first place, if genuine knowledge were confined to immaterial
entities we should possess no understanding of bodies in motion.
There would be no science of matter in change. In the second
place in order to understand objects we are asked to refer to
entities which have no connexion with them.

It is error to believe that the understanding is constituted so as
not to know bodies. Universality is indeed the characteristic of
thought, but the objects of thought need not exist also as universals. The form of the thing known need not be in the knower in the
same way. The sensible form exists in the real world outside the
mind in one way; it appears in another way in the mental apprehension of it. And the understanding grasps in its own way the
species of bodies. They are material and in motion; in the understanding they become immaterial amd motionless. Yet it is knowledge of them and not of another order of being. For what is
received is in the receiver according to the nature of the receiver.[2]

[1] Q. lxxxv. 2.   [2] Q. lxxxiv. 1; cf. ib. 6.

But let us now proceed to elucidate more closely the manner in which understanding co-operates with sense in the act of awareness.

VI

For human beings the forms of objects are embodied in particular material things. The forms, the essences of things, have accordingly to be grasped indirectly, by activities which supervene upon sensation. The contents presented by the outer and inner senses are particular, and so they cannot provide of themselves the objects of knowledge. For the mind, or in Thomas's language the possible intellect, receives only universal species. A purely particular entity is an abstraction; it could not be an object of consciousness. It is necessary, then, that the contents of sensory apprehension should be extracted from their material setting, stripped of their unique determinations, in order to become items of thought. In a word, the sensory particulars have to be made general. This process is performed by the active understanding or intellect, *intellectus agens*.

Thomas is fond of comparing its function to that of light. As the colours of objects are made visible for the eye by light, so material entities are rendered intelligible by the active intellect. It reveals objects by illuminating the phantasms.[1] It is an active not a passive power. It is not provoked by the action of bodies on the mind; it exhibits the action of the mind on bodies. The mind produces itself the force by which it is enlightened. Knowledge is not wholly derived from sensory factors, though they play their part.

The activity of the *intellectus agens* is manifested in the constant movement of thought from the concrete to the abstract, from the ideas implicit in the bare apprehensions of external objects to general notions of science and philosophy. The more abstract the object of thought the nobler and higher it is in itself.[2]

The active intellect is not a power outside the mind, an Intelligence in which the mind can share. For it is imperfect and attains truth, not by direct intuition, but by a process of inquiry and partial approaches, in fact by reasoning. The Augustinian view that the active intellect is the divine Mind must be rejected.[3] The limitations of our minds, the ideals to which knowledge points, and the teaching of Faith, lead us to believe in a substantially separate and supreme Intelligence. But the active intellect is human. It is

[1] Q. lxxix.   [2] Q. lxxxii.   [3] Q. lxxix. 4.

a power not of Mind, but of minds. Many minds are not in reality one mind as Realism had maintained. There are as many active intellects as there are men.[1]

The primary work of the active intellect is to make general and so apprehensible the disappearing and disconnected *phantasmata* of sensory experience. It performs this in Thomas's terms by abstracting the intelligible species from the *phantasmata*. The significance of *species intelligibilis* in Thomas's scheme is complex and difficult. It is a form, that is to say it is an immanent activity which expresses the nature of the knowing subject. But it also expresses the nature of the object. It is an emanation or likeness of the object which is fitted by its physical character to combine with mind and produce the act of awareness. For objects cannot enter our minds in concrete form. In order that apprehension should occur the object must meet our mind without ceasing to be itself and at the same time without physical invasion of the mind. The species is the ideal intermediary which unites object and subject in the act of consciousness.

Accordingly it is not an object of thought; it is that by which we think. What we apprehend is the object, this house, or justice, not the way in which we apprehend. Theories of representative thinking are ruled out by this interpretation of the species. Our knowledge is directly concerned with external realities, not with representations of them. But it can grasp external objects only by freeing the intelligible form which is implicit in them.[2] In the realm of spirit mind corresponds to pure matter in the world of physical being. It is potency, indetermination, unintelligent. It can only become intelligent when it is informed by the intelligible species of a body.

The intelligible species is a principle of unity. The mind can only perform at one time a single act of understanding. It embraces many objects or elements in one perspective. The presence of several intelligible species necessarily means several acts of consciousness.[3] Our knowledge of relations rests on this principle. Take, for example, the relation of whole and part. If we attend to the parts by themselves the whole recedes from view; each part constitutes a whole in its turn. If, on the contrary, we consider the whole the parts are apprehended only in a vague manner as existing in the whole.[4] Or take the perception of the difference between objects, or the process of comparing them. It is true that

[1] Q. lxxix. 4, 5; lxxvi. 2. [2] Q. lxxxv. 2. [3] Q. lxxxv. 4. [4] Ib. ad 3.

the mind must know both the objects at the same time in order to distinguish and compare them. But the terms of these judgements are not known separately in themselves, but in relation to the judgement of comparing or distinguishing.[1] In any judgement, in fact, the parts of the proposition, the subject and the predicate, are not understood as distinct items. It is the proposition as a whole which is understood. All the parts are known according to a single species of the whole.[2]

Besides introducing unity into the *phantasmata* the active intellect in bringing to light the intelligible species generalizes the sensible images. Thomas describes abstraction in language closely resembling that of Abaelard, for here as at every stage of his philosophical reflections he was obliged to guard his doctrine from the current teachings of extreme Realism. In thinking of the qualities of objects we do not refer to items which have distinct existence. In abstraction we attend to aspects of things in isolation from other aspects. This separation occurs on the perceptual level of experience.

'For if we mean or assert that colour is not in the coloured object or that it exists separately from it, there would be error in thought or expression. But if we consider colour and its properties without at all referring in our minds to the coloured apple, or if we express what we think, there will be no error either of thought or expression. For the apple is not essential to the colour. There is no difficulty in thinking of the colour without thinking of the apple. In the same way I maintain that the features which essentially belong to the species of any material object, such as a stone or a man or a horse, can be thought of apart from the individual characteristics which do not belong essentially to the species. And this is what is meant by abstracting the universal from the particular or the intelligible species from the phantasms. The species is thought of apart from the individual principles which the phantasms represent.'[3]

There are two points here. In thought we attend to features cut loose as it were from the objects in which they inhere. And these features are general; we do not mean by colour the image of any particular colour we may have in our minds when we think of colour.

Thomas gives a brief survey of various levels of abstraction. Abstraction may be of the general or of the particular. We may think of flesh and bones in general or of some particular flesh and

---

[1] Q. lxxxv. 4 ad 4.   [2] Cont. Gent. i. 55.   [3] Q. lxxxv. 1 ad 1.

bones. Now the active intellect abstracts the species of an object from particular sensible matter, not from sensible matter in general. The notion of a man is formed from some particular flesh and bones. But it is possible to abstract species from matter in general. General features of matter are qualities such as cold and hot, hard and soft. This is we may presume the province of physics. But the mind can proceed further in the realm of the abstract. It can descry an order beyond the general sensibles. Now this is substance as subject to quantity, and Thomas names it intelligible matter. Quantity is prior to other sensible forms. Quantities, for example number, dimension, and figure, can be treated apart from other sensible qualities. Finally we may take a further step, beyond intelligible or mathematical matter. All that now remains for our thought are elements such as being, unity, potency, and act. These can be studies apart from all matter. Here we reach the province of metaphysics.[1]

The *species intelligibilis* is thus made explicit and becomes the *species intellecta*, the general object or concept of which the mind is conscious. Thomas is accustomed to refer to it as *verbum* or expression, thus emphasizing the intimate connexion between thinking and language. The language, however, may be interior, *verbum cordis*. The concept is directed to being expressed either to oneself or to others; and Thomas accordingly excludes 'simple intuition' or 'implicit apprehension' from conception.[2] A general term is a similitude of an actual thing, not, of course, the likeness which holds between the intelligible species and the object, but a resemblance existing between an ideational representation and concrete individual thing. The likeness has only intentional being. It is not a thing, nor is it in things. It is a way of comprehending things to which we are compelled by the deficiencies of our understandings.

The immediate foundation of the general ideas which form the main texture of our thought is not in things but in the mind. What the mind knows are abstractions. The particularity of things can never be seized. Conceptual thought is indistinct. 'It is evident that to apprehend an object that comprises many things, without proper knowledge of each thing contained in it, is to apprehend that object in a confused way.[3] The senses have intuitions; thought strives after intuitions but must be content with partial views of reality. This human knowledge is midway between the

---

[1] Ib. ad 2.
[2] In IV libri Sententiarum, i, d. 27, q. 2, a 1.   [3] Q. lxxxv. 3.

potentiality of conceptual thought and perfect act, the intellectual intuition of objects, which is the prerogative of the angels.

Thomas frequently asserts that the natural object of the human mind is the 'quiddity' or essence of a material thing.[1] Yet to these affirmations must be joined statements which seem directly to contradict this position. Thus he often says that the essences of things are unknown to us. The contradiction appears sometimes in the same article. The solution of the antinomy must be sought in an analysis of the structure of the intelligible form. What is first known by mind is being, to which it refers all its conceptions. All other conceptions of the understanding must be arrived at by an addition to that which is.[2] We understand being in ways which variously qualify it. Thus we break the unity of being, piecing it into genera and species, into classes and things. On the other hand, we preserve the indeterminate unity of being, but only by expressing general modes which are no being in particular, such as unity, real, good. But all being possesses both special and general modes. We attain then the essence immediately, in so far as we apprehend the general features before the particular.[3] And the mind in apprehending the quiddity in this sense is always apprehending the truth.[4] It is in conformity with reality.

But the truth is not consciously seen to be truth until the mind distinguishes between itself and the objects of its thought. It asks how far its conceptions, arbitrarily abstracted from experience, conform to experience.

'But the understanding forming quiddities has only the likeness of the thing existing outside the mind, as sense has in so far as it receives the species of the sensible thing. When, however, it begins to judge concerning the thing apprehended, then the very judgement of the understanding is something proper to it which is not found outside the thing. But when it is adequated to that which is outside the thing, the judgement is said to be true.'

The concept which is produced by the operation of the active intellect has, as we have seen, a counterpart immanent in particular things. Truth is the conformity of the mind with this pervading form.

VII

There is a passage in the *Summa Theologica*[5] in which Thomas defines his position on the nature of knowledge in relation to

---

[1] Cf. Q. lxxxv. 5. [2] De Ver. Q. i. 1. [3] Q. lxxxv. 3.
[4] De Ver. i. 3. [5] Q. lxxxiv. 6.

sensationalism on the one hand and Augustinian idealism on the other. We cannot conclude our brief survey of his philosophy of knowledge more appropriately than by presenting the argument of this passage. It clearly epitomizes the Thomistic account of knowledge.

He begins, as usual, by stating several of the texts which reject the position for which he proposes to argue. The traditional texts are naturally drawn from St. Augustine. In the work named *Eighty-three Problems* he had asserted that genuine truth cannot be sought for in the bodily senses. For, in the first place, whatever the bodily senses reach is in process of continual change. And what has no permanence cannot be perceived. In the second place everything which we perceive through the body, even when it is not present to the senses, may be apprehended by us in the form of images. This occurs when we are asleep or in a state of excitement. But we cannot distinguish, so long as we rely on the senses, whether what we are perceiving are sensible objects or illusory images of them. Augustine concludes that we cannot seek the truth in the senses. Yet we do, in thought (*cognitio intellectualis*), apprehend the truth. Therefore it cannot rely upon sense-experience.

These are typical Platonic arguments against sensationalism. The objects of sensation are evanescent, and it is impossible to distinguish percepts from images. But Augustine assumes that perception is composed of sensations, and he therefore severs it from thought. Thomas now quotes the passage from Augustine in which he asserts that the mind produces the counterpart of impressions from its own substance.[1] 'It is inconceivable', he had said, 'that the body can make any impression on the mind, as though the mind were a substitute for matter in the activities of the body. For that which acts is in every way superior to that which is subject to action.' Hence he inferred that the bodily image is not produced in the mind by the body, but the mind itself causes it to arise within itself. Intellectual knowledge is not therefore derived from sensible objects.

He adds a further objection drawn from a prevailing precept of medieval thought. No effect surpasses its cause in power. But intellectual knowledge extends further than knowledge of sensible objects, for we have understanding of things which cannot be perceived by the senses, and so it cannot be a consequent sensation.

[1] Gen. ad. lit. xii. 16. Cf. p. 13 above.

He concludes his preliminary citation of opinions by a contrary statement from Aristotle that the foundation of our knowledge is in the senses.

Thomas now proceeds to discuss the question as follows. Three views have been held by philosophers on this problem. Democritus maintained that the only cause of our knowledge are images which flow from the bodies of which we are aware and pass into our minds, as Augustine records in his letter to Dioscorus.[1] Aristotle also says in his work *On Prophecy in Sleep* that Democritus held that knowledge takes place by means of images and fluxions emanating from objects. And the reason for this theory was that both Democritus and the other ancient natural philosophers did not consider that thought can be distinguished from sensation, as Aristotle points out in his treatise *On Mind*. In consequence, since sensation is a response to sensible entities, these philosophers thought that all our knowledge can be reduced to the impression of sensible entities on the mind. And this impression Democritus maintained was brought about by discharges of images from objects.

Plato, on the other hand, held that thought is distinct from sensation. He considered it to be an immaterial power which makes no use of a bodily organ. And since what is without body cannot be affected by body, he held that intellectual knowledge does not take place through the operation of sensible objects on the intellect, but in virtue of the intellect's participation in separate intelligible forms. He held further that sensation is a self-active power. It follows that sensation, since it is a spiritual power, is not a response to sensible objects; it is only the organs of sensation which are affected by sensible objects. In virtue of this distinction we can say that the mind is moved to form within itself the species of sensible entities. Thomas here recalls Augustine's doctrine which we have discussed above,[2] that it is not the body which experiences sensation but the mind through the body. The mind uses the body in the manner of a messenger in order to produce in itself what is announced from outside. He concludes his summary of the Platonic position thus. On the one hand, thought does not spring from sensation; on the other hand, sensation does not wholly arise from the impressions of sensible objects. Sensible objects excite the sensitive level of the mind to experience sensation, and in the same way sensations produce intellectual activity in the intellectual part of the mind.

[1] Ep. cxviii; P.L. xxxiii. 446. [2] p. 14 above.

But there is a middle course open to us between sensationalism and Platonism and it is this middle course which, Thomas points out, was adopted by Aristotle. He agreed with Plato in distinguishing between thought and sensation. But he held that sensation cannot actually take place apart from the co-operation of the body. Sensation is not the activity of the mind alone, but the activity of the complex being, the body-mind. And this is true of all the activities of the sensory part of the mind. It is to be expected that the sensible objects outside the mind should produce some effect on the composite entity. Accordingly Aristotle so far agreed with Democritus that he considered the activities of the sensory part of the mind are caused by the impression of the sensible object; though he held that this took place not by an influx of atoms, but by a peculiar type of activity appropriate to the body-mind. But intellectual activity he thought was independent of the body's activity. Now nothing material can make any impression on an entity which is immaterial, and therefore, according to Aristotle, in order to bring about intellectual activity the mere impression of material sensible objects is not sufficient, but a higher form of process is necessary. For that which is active is nobler than that which is passive. But in subscribing to this principle Thomas adds that it does not follow that the intellectual activity is caused only by the impression on our minds of a higher order of reality. This was the view of Plato. The meaning is that the higher and nobler activity of which Aristotle speaks, and which is in fact the active intellect which has been discussed above, causes the images received from the senses to be expressed by a process of abstraction.

Thought, or intellectual activity, depends on sensation. But images cannot of themselves affect the mind.[1] They become intelligible through the work of the active intellect. Consequently it is impossible to maintain that sensory knowledge is the whole cause of thought; it is rather the material cause or occasion.

Such is Thomas's doctrine. The sensory and generalizing factors in perception are aspects of a process which includes them both. This complex activity is in part dependent upon physical stimulus, in part upon a preliminary grasp of the physical particulars by the mind. This process is one of generalization and from it spring reflection on abstract qualities and beings. When I perceive a pen the particular physical forces which impinge on the eye are

---

[1] *intellectus possibilis.*

apprehended in the form of a particular image, and this is necessary in order that the perception to take place. But it is not this
changing image which I perceive, but the object. And this has
general features. The pen possesses permanence and continuity,
and the qualities which are perceived in it, its brown colour, shape,
and hardness are implicitly abstract notions capable of being
further abstracted from their particular embodiment in the pen.
But before we proceed to describe Thomas's account of the non-
sensory components of experience let us complete our description
of the present section. What remains are the replies to the objections quoted at the beginning of the article.

To the first, that sensation gives no permanence, and that if
there were nothing but sensation it would be impossible to
distinguish between perceptions and illusions, Thomas briefly
replies, that all Augustine means is that truth or real knowledge is
not to be sought in sensory experience. The light of the active
intellect is also required. And by it we apprehend the unchanging
truth amid changing entities; and are enabled to distinguish real
objects from illusory images.

To the second objection Thomas replies thus. When Augustine
asserts that the mind produces images from within itself and is not
affected by physical forces, he is referring not to thought but to
imagination. But according to Plato imagination is a process
which takes place only in the mind. Augustine follows this view in
order to point out that bodies do not impress their images on the
imagination, but that it is only the mind which does this. Here he
employs the same argument as does Aristotle when he seeks to show
that the active intellect is a separate process, the argument namely
that what is active is superior in nature to what is passive. It is
clear that, according to this position, we must assign to the imagination not only a passive but also an active role. But if we hold
with Aristotle that the activity of imagination is an activity of the
composite being, the body-mind, there is no difficulty. For the
sensible body is superior to the animal organ, in that the former
is related to the latter as what is in act to what is in potency, just
as what is actually coloured is related to the pupil of the eye, which
is only potentially coloured. It may be said, however, that although
the primary effect of the imagination occurs by means of motions
on the part of the sensible objects, since, as Aristotle says, the
awareness of images is motion in accordance with sense, yet there
is in man a mental activity which forms various images of things by

analysis and synthesis, even of things which are not perceived by the senses. It is possible, Thomas concludes, to interpret Augustine's works in this sense.

These replies to the objections cited from Augustine illustrate Thomas's custom of adapting the Platonism of the great Church Father so as to avoid conflict with his own position. But it is doubtful whether Augustine can be interpreted in this way. For him sensation is a mental parallel of physical stimulus and apprehends the stimulus directly.

In reply to the third point Thomas observes that sensory awareness is not the whole basis of thought. Hence it is not strange that thought should surpass sensation in range.

VIII

Thomas founds knowledge upon sensible experience. But he gives no encouragement to the development of scientific investigation. He is respectful towards natural knowledge and echoing Augustine[1] he warns Christians against displaying their ignorance in discussing scientific questions. He lays down the principle that Holy Scripture can be explained in a number of ways and no one should abide by any particular interpretation so rigidly as to be unwilling to abandon it if it should clearly be shown to be false. Otherwise Scripture is exposed to the ridicule of unbelievers and obstacles placed in the way of their assent to the Faith.[2] The Angelic doctor is credited with a work of irrigation and mechanical engineering. But it is plain that his interest in empirical inquiry was meagre. He adopts without question the cosmology of Aristotle, the concentric spheres of the four elements, earth, water, air, and fire, the unchanging celestial spheres beyond the terrestrial order. He believed in demons, witchcraft, and divination, though he distinguished magic from legitimate science. But in two ways he prepared opinion, by criticizing prevailing error, to attend to the phenomena of nature. The errors which he strove to defeat were the refusal to recognize the independent working of secondary causes, and the belief that Nature was evil.

God is the ultimate cause of all the processes of nature. But Thomas does not agree with those theologians who, in the light of this premiss, tended to exclude and belittle the action of natural causation. He refuses to attribute the cause of heat to God and not to the fire. He traces this denial of natural efficiency to the

----

[1] Cf. p. 19 above.　　　　[2] Q. lxviii. 1.

influence of Platonism, for in conformity with the theological view of nature Platonism had ascribed causal sequences to immaterial forms separated from the sensible realm. A similar opinion was held by Moslem theologians. Thus from many quarters direct interest in the operations of nature was disparaged.

Thomas attacks the orthodox view on the following grounds. If the action of all bodies on one another is due to nothing but the work of God, no effects appropriate to the special nature of things would necessarily follow. For God suffers no change through working by means of different creatures, and He could cause any effect to follow any cause. Actually, however, we see a uniform sequence of causes and effects; a hot body invariably produces heat and not cold, a human being always generates another human being. The necessary sequence of nature would be incomprehensible and otiose if God were the direct cause of all phenomena. Indeed such a view, in disparaging nature, disparages God; for if nothing effects anything, the world, which is the creation of God, becomes valueless. If the genuine interaction of things is not recognized we deny any order in the world, for the only way in which things radically different from one another form an order is through being connected by cause and effect. To attribute all effects not to things but to the immediate action of God makes it impossible to detect a cause from an examination of its effects, and thus all natural science is denied us.

A further point is that an effect in the realm of nature is a composite of matter and form; it is not simply form. But on the rule that like is produced by like the cause also must be not a form but a composite being. It must be a particular thing composed of matter and form. The distinct species of the Platonists and the active intellect as conceived by Avicenna must both be rejected as accounts of natural cause, since both are purely formal principles.[1]

But no medieval philosopher would deny that, however strongly the operation of secondary causes is insisted on, God is also present in the activities of nature. No difficulty, Thomas points out, arises from admitting both types of causation if certain distinctions are borne in mind. We must distinguish in every activity the thing which is active and the force in virtue of which it is active. A fire is a thing which is active in virtue of its heat. Now the effective power of a thing which is active is dependent on the power of an

[1] Contra Gent. iii. 69.

activity beyond it. Thus a craftsman directs a tool to its proper use. The lower agent, the instrument, is none the less a genuine and immediate cause of the effect, though it does not act, except under the control of the higher agent. The application to the divine activity in the natural universe is easily seen. Nature is God's instrument. He is the primary cause, the impact of things upon one another is the secondary cause. The most trivial event produces its special effects, but it is only able to do this in virtue of all the superior causes to which it is subject. But the analogy between God's relation to the world and that of a craftsman to his instrument must not be pressed too far. God is not external to the world, as a craftsman is external to his tool. The causal sequences of nature reveal, says St. Thomas, the immensity of God's goodness. He has communicated His Being to the multiplicity of events; and every natural activity exists, not for its own sake, but as a manifestation of the divine Life.[1]

Thomas is never tired of demonstrating the goodness of nature. And here it is important to appreciate the circumstances under which he wrote. In attacking the assumption that nature is evil he is not merely criticizing a perverse theory. He is concerned with the greatest danger that ever assailed the Medieval Church. The thirteenth century saw a widespread revival of Manichaean beliefs, against which, as we have noticed, Augustine had strenuously fought. The most notorious example of this rigid Puritan creed was the Albigensian heresy, on which the Church had exacted such terrible punishment. But the heresy had been almost as general as the Catholic Faith. The doctrines of this movement were based upon a dualism of spirit and matter, and it was believed that all forms of matter were evil. Nature, including the bodies of animals and men, was indiscriminatingly condemned. The Albigenses rejected the fundamental doctrines of orthodox Christianity and advocated social practices which threatened the continuance of the human race.

In his refutation of this pessimistic view of nature, which he traces back to Origen, Thomas rests upon a belief in the organic character of reality. We must think of the universe as an organic whole, in which all the parts contribute to the whole. In the attempt to discern the purpose of any particular unity or its parts, we find that each part exists for the sake of its particular function. Thus the eyes exist for the purpose of seeing. We observe further

[1] Ib. 70.

H

that the less important parts exist for the sake of the more important. The senses, for example, serve thought, and the lungs the heart. We see, too, that all parts are directed to the perfection of the whole, in the way in which matter serves form. Indeed, parts may be deemed matter in relation to the whole which can be conceived as form. If we now think of man as a whole we must look beyond him to the end which he serves. And this is the enjoyment of God.

Every creature, then, in the universe exists for the performance of its function. The inferior exists for the sake of the superior, and in the end every created thing exists to serve the entire universe. And reaching further Thomas asserts that the universe of nature with all its parts tends towards God. The divine goodness is the goal of all material things.[1]

IX

In sum, then, the progress of thought is the effort to realize the ideal unity which is the common ground of mind and its objects. It is an endeavour, the goal of which is fulfilment of being, and accordingly it is a facet of the all-pervading rhythm of potency and act. The understanding and what is understood are fundamentally of the same order. The movement of the spirit in the process of knowledge, in the process that is to say of identifying itself with its objects, constitutes the activity of the *species intelligibilis*. This approach of mind to its objects is expressed in various modes of unity by which general being is grasped, modes such as existence and essence, substance and accidents, genera and species. St. Thomas extends and deepens the notion of universals to include these primordial forms of being, which are the necessary conditions of awareness of objects. Accordingly he maintains that the mind apprehends universals directly, particulars indirectly. And the oft-repeated assertion that the proper object of the mind is the *nature* of some material thing expresses the same doctrine.

But this apprehension of universals in material things is an awareness of extremely general features, of thinghood or being or oneness. In the effort to understand things more nearly, whether they be men, or trees, or rocks, we are led to specify and define the implicit universals. And here the human mind is limited by the presence of matter which confronts it at every turn. The universal element is in itself intelligible, and provides insight into the

[1] Q. lxv. 2.

foundation of things. But it is never found in itself. Thomas criticizes Platonism, that is to say the extreme Realism of the Medieval School, from every angle. We can only know Form directly in matter, and this means that it is always for us immersed in particular things. The intellectual element in mind cannot grasp particulars, for they are in themselves unintelligible. They are apprehended by corporeal organs through the senses of our bodies. Sensory awareness or perception is a condition of further understanding of the nature of things; and this further exploration of universal principles, of genera and species and of other relations is obtained by the process of abstraction and comparison. This is the work of the *intellectus agens*, which disengages universals from their sensory expression. The conceptions which we thus construct, ever reaching for more concrete universals, are likenesses of things. They are phenomena. We cannot attain the essences of things, for our dependence on perception compels our thought to be discursive.

Thus Thomas stands midway between extreme Realism and Nominalism. Whiteness and colour are reached by a process of analysis and synthesis, and must fall short of the concrete reality known in perception. In comparison the genera and species of thought and science are appearances, and exist *quoad modum concipiendi*. The modes of thought by which the mind understands the world differ from the mode of being in which nature exists. But the implicit universals which are given in sensible things and the abstract universals of reflection are not collections of sense-impressions nor mental signs by which singular images are conventionally taken to apply to a class. Our concepts refer to a universality in things though not apart from things. The business of discovering what are the essential characteristics of things demands an incessant revision of our abstractions. It requires a perpetual reference to the data of perception and a constant pursuit of logical coherence. St. Thomas is not concerned with working out a logic of empirical investigation. Duns Scotus pursued this problem. But the final lesson of his philosophy of knowledge is that human understanding is based upon sensory experience and that intuition of intelligible realities is impossible. The task of thought is to approach the complex realm of things by many paths, and so draw nearer to the concrete universal where essence and understanding are one. But we can never pass beyond similitudes. The proper object of thought is the knowledge of Form in matter. Such a position is capable of providing a foundation for natural science, while extreme Realism and Nominalism assuredly cannot do so. Nevertheless the theory of knowledge is an incidental feature in the vast edifice of the *Summa Theologica*. The theme of St. Thomas's tremendous work is Sacred Doctrine, a science which is higher in dignity than other speculative sciences.[1] The impulse to develop scientific methods was not derived from the greatest of the Schoolmen, though beyond all other medieval thinkers his philosophical teaching was destined to endure.

Q i. a 5.

WILLIAM OF OCKHAM

REFERENCES

There are no modern editions of the philosophical works of William of Ockham. *The Commentary on the Sentences* has not been reprinted since 1495; the latest edition of the *Summa Totius Logicae* is the Oxford edition of 1675. The chief sources for the following account are the references in N. Abbagnano, *Guglielmo di Ockham*, Lanciano, 1931; S. C. Tornay, *Ockham, Studies and Selections*, La Salle, 1938; R. McKeon, *Selections from Medieval Philosophers*, London, 1931, vol. ii, pp. 351–421; E. A. Moody, *The Logic of William of Ockham*, London, 1935; E. Gilson, *The Unity of Philosophical Experience*, London, 1938; and the extensive quotations in C. Prantl, *Geschichte der Logik im Abendlande*, 1867, vol. iii, cap. 19. Abbagnano gives a useful bibliography up to 1930. A work of doubtful authenticity, *De Principiis Theologicae*, has been edited by L. Baudry, Paris, 1936.

I

IN the fourteenth century medieval philosophy began to disintegrate. The decline in thought was part of the general collapse of the old order of Christendom to which many factors contributed. Among these events were the public scandals in the Church, the Hundred Years War, and the Black Death. A period of moral confusion set in, and mental activity deteriorated. Confidence in reason decreased, and an era of scepticism and theological irrationalism ensued. One mark of the destructive forces of the time was the revival of Nominalism, the chief advocate of which was William of Ockham.

He was born about the year 1300 at the village of Ockham near Guildford in Surrey. At an early age he became a student at Oxford, and soon afterwards entered the Franciscan Order. He completed his course at Oxford as far as the Bachelor stage, and taught there until 1324. But he never attained to the degree of Master in Theology. Students who did not proceed beyond the

The abbreviations refer to the following works:

Cent. Theolog.	Centilogium Theologicum.
Expos. Aur.	Expositio Aurea et admodum utilis super artem veterem.
Quodlib.	Quodlibeta septem.
Sum. tot. log.	Summa totius logicae.
Summulae	Summulae in libros physicorum.
Sent.	Super quatuor libros sententiarum subtilissimae quaestiones earundumque decisiones.

Bachelor stage of the degree were known as *inceptores*, and Ockham became renowned as the *venerabilis inceptor*. It is probable that the originality of his views even at this early period of his life was disapproved of by the Doctors of the University. Certainly the vigour with which he announced them soon brought him into dis-favour in the highest quarter. It had long been customary for a teacher in philosophy to enter on his career with a course of lectures on the Four Books of *Sentences* of Peter Lombard. This work, which was composed about 1150, is a collection of the opinions of the Church Fathers, especially those of St. Augustine, upon the principal topics of theology. It had become the chief text-book of the University, and Roger Bacon declared that at Paris the *Sentences* were more studied than the Bible. The lectures of the young *inceptor* proved to be dangerously unorthodox; he propounded a doctrine of empiricism, and did not shrink from objecting to the grounds upon which the tenets of theology were traditionally supported. His doctrines were referred to the Curia; and in 1324 he was summoned by the Pope to Avignon in order to face an investigation of his opinions. Judgement was delayed, and for some years William was confined in the Franciscan house at Avignon.

But meanwhile the provocative young scholar had become prominent in a more formidable controversy. The Pope, the ruth-less and avaricious John XXII, had attempted to suppress the teaching of the mendicant party of the Franciscans, a body which believed in and practised the doctrine of the absolute poverty of Christ. The movement was bitterly hostile to the Papacy, nor could the tortures of the Inquisition check its rapid growth in north Italy and France. In a sermon delivered at Bologna, Ockham publicly allied himself with these spirituals, who were led by the general of the Franciscan Order, Michael of Cesena. He was arrested and imprisoned at Avignon. In 1326 a commission of six theolo-gians found that fifty-one articles in his commentary on the *Sentences* were heretical and pestilential. But Ockham refused to retract them, and in 1328 added to the danger of his position by signing the protest drawn up by Cesena against the Papal Bull which had condemned the doctrine of apostolic poverty. On the night of 24 May of that year, in company with Cesena and Bona-gratia, the brilliant Franciscan lawyer, he escaped from the prison at Avignon and made a perilous journey to Pisa. Here he placed himself under the protection of the Emperor, Louis of Bavaria. By this action he finally severed himself from the authority of the Pope. In the previous year Louis had descended on Rome, proclaimed the deposition of John XXII, and set up an anti-Pope of his own election. Ockham was solemnly excommunicated upon joining himself with the monarch against whom the Pope had already exhausted his spiritual maledictions.

Soon after this critical event in Ockham's career the Emperor and his court moved to Munich. The youthful philosopher had promised to defend Louis with his pen in return for the protection of the Emperor's sword; and now from the seclusion of the Franciscan monastery at Munich he poured forth a series of pamphlets directed against the Pope. The most important of these are the *Eight Questions concerning the Power and Dignity of the Pope* and the *Dialogue between Master and Disciples upon the Power of Emperors and Popes*. His main purpose in these works is to advocate a loftier discipline for the Church, but he expresses a remarkable defence of the principle of political representation both in Church and State. In conformity with his theory of knowledge he placed the emphasis upon the individual person in opposition to the corporate body; and he asserts that the actions of the State must be judged according to the law of nature. He finds the seat of the law of nature in the moral decisions of individual citizens. In such reflections he lent assistance to the reforming ideas of his great contemporary, Marsilio of Padua, the author of *Defensor Pacis*.

Ockham remained at Munich engaged in polemical writing in every field of discussion. He produced a comprehensive logical treatise entitled *Summa totius logicae*. During these years he was compelled to witness the decline of his protector's resolution. The Emperor entered into negotiations with Pope Benedict XXII. He wrote pitiful excuses for his past action and foreswore all his former partisans. Among these was Cesena with whose cause Ockham had been so deeply identified. Ockham took part in the numerous Diets of prelates, princes, and nobles which met to discuss the reconciliation of the Empire and the Papacy, and it is possible to detect the influence of his ideas in a declaration which asserted that the right of electing the Emperor was independent of the approbation of the Pope. But after numerous vacillations Louis, in 1344, agreed to the most humiliating terms at the hands of Clement VI. He was deserted by his supporters and died in 1347. Amid the tribulations caused by these events Ockham had also to endure the devastation spread by the Black Death, and in 1349 he himself succumbed to the plague.

William of Ockham was a revolutionary figure. His life was spent in polemics. His logical criticisms shook the foundations of Scholasticism, and the dialectics of the following centuries revolved round the problems which he had raised. His three most important philosophical works are the *Commentary on the Sentences*, the *Sum of All Logic*, and the *Golden Exposition of the Ancient Art*. Let us now proceed to indicate the circumstances in which these works were composed.

II

Thomas Aquinas died in 1274. The remaining quarter of the thirteenth century was filled with controversies excited by his challenge to the accepted views, and the current of thought for a time prevailed against the new Aristotelianism. Three years after the death of Thomas, the Bishop of Paris received instructions from the Pope to make an inquiry into the doctrines taught at the University. The Bishop found himself obliged to condemn no less than two hundred and nineteen theses maintained in the schools; and though the bulk of the censored propositions were Averroistic, a number of important doctrines taught by Thomas were also included in the ban. The ascription of the principle of individuation to matter, for instance, and the teaching that the body participated in the intellectual operations of the mind, were forbidden. A few days after the decree of Paris a similar condemnation of Thomist theories was declared at Oxford. This indictment of certain principles of the new school was the signal for renewed confidence in Augustinian ideas, and a number of Franciscan philosophers asserted the traditional theory of knowledge and reality in opposition to the Thomist philosophy.

For Augustine our conceptions are not obtained by recourse to objects perceived by the senses; the mind illumined by the divine Light directly apprehends the immutable truth in the eternal reasons. To the problem of abstraction Augustine, as we have seen, gives no clear answer.[1] Accordingly philosophers who held that he was the teacher *par excellence*, philosophers such as Matthew of Aquasparta[2] and Roger Marston, attempted a compromise between

[1] Cf. p. 17 above.

[2] Matthew of Aquasparta was born about 1240 and died in 1302. He was a pupil of Bonaventura and was general of the Franciscan Order in 1287. The references to his views are taken from *Quaestiones de Fide et Cognitione*, Q. 2.

the doctrines of their master and the analysis of knowledge presented in the new system. Matthew agreed that Thomas's account of knowledge as the production of sense, memory, and experience, and that the description of the way in which the active intellect abstracts the intelligible species from the sensory images, furnished an adequate representation of the processes of temporal knowledge or *scientia*. But he refused to admit that *scientia* was the whole of knowledge. Our knowledge has *a priori* as well as an *a posteriori* source; and certain demonstrations, those for example which lead to proofs of God's existence and of the spiritual nature of the self, are open to it apart from sense-experience. But Matthew adds a curiously Kantian interpretation to the 'ideal reasons'. They are not objects of our thought, but motives which lead and direct our understanding. 'The material principle of knowing is from external things from which the species of the things to be known are derived, but the formal principle is partly within, that is from the light of reason, partly from above, but fully and finally from the eternal rules and reasons.' Roger Marston held that the active intellect is nothing but the divine illumination in which we perceive with certitude all the truth implicit in our judgements of reality. Thus in the face of Thomas's arguments the characteristic position of Augustine was reaffirmed.

Many other writers contributed to this reassertion of the older view of knowledge. Even Roger Bacon,[1] despite his eloquent advocacy of experimental methods, insisted that they must be supplemented by inner illumination. He argued at length against the view that the active intellect is part of the mind. It is, he averred, a substance separate from the mind subject to the divine inspiration. And in other respects he adhered to the principles of Neoplatonism.

But the end of the century produced a young philosopher of greater power and ingenuity than any of these authorities; one of the pre-eminent thinkers of the Middle Ages. 'Subtle' is the traditional and appropriate epithet applied to Duns Scotus.[2] The interpretation of his views is difficult; but he appears on some

[1] Roger Bacon was born about 1215 and lectured at Paris and at Oxford. His works contain extraordinarily prophetic conclusions on such matters as plant-life, the habits of animals, the nature of tides and rainbows, and the density of the air. He sketched the principles of an embracing science which should bring all natural phenomena under mathematical principles. He died in 1294.

[2] He was born about 1270 in Scotland, studied at Cambridge and at Oxford, frequently visited Paris, and died at Cologne in 1308.

issues to range himself in opposition to the doctrines of St. Thomas. Thus he rejects the distinction between essence and existence, and refuses to admit the Thomist view of matter as pure potency. For our purpose, the modifications which he introduced into the new theory of knowledge are of interest. He agrees with Thomas in recognizing that all knowledge springs from sensory apprehension of particular entities. This perceptual apprehension is, however, complex, corresponding to the complexity of the individual thing. The mind discovers a number of formal elements in the objective world, in the light of which particular things are *formalitates*, perceived and understood. Causal connexion is one of these principles. We shall find that Ockham criticizes this view of knowledge, which resembles that of Kant, as a variety of extreme Realism. Yet Scotus also refuses to accept principles dear to the followers of Augustine, and considers the doctrine of Illumination an invitation to scepticism.

Thus at the close of the century resistance to Thomism was strong. Thomas indeed had many disciples, and his prestige was established by the support of the Dominican Order. But the revival of Augustinian interpretations of knowledge throughout the universities inspired much of the polemics of William of Ockham.

And there is another less negative tradition of which William was the heir. We have seen that Abaelard in the twelfth century founded a school of logicians who directed their attention to the relation between thought and language.[1] A conspicuous writer in this field was Petrus Hispanus (1226–77), who in his *Summulae Logicales* discusses at length the properties of words. He treats of words as signs, the expansion and restriction of signs; the principles of naming and other properties of terms. The connexions of logical thinking are regarded as ways in which words can be arranged. Many philosophers were led to investigate, after Petrus, 'the modes of signification'. These teachers concentrated more upon correct expression than upon truth. For them metaphysical questions concerning the nature of the objects to which terms refer became matters of secondary interest. When the principle consideration is the way in which things are understood and expressed, the path is open for a development of conceptualism and nominalism. Thus a typical utterance of this school is the following: 'It is clear that the notion of man and of animal in so far as it is distinguished from Socrates is a fabrication of the intellect

[1] p. 65 above.

and is nothing but a concept; for nature has not formed distinct principles of this kind as actual existences.'[1] Here are Conceptualism and Nominalism in a sentence. The generality in our thinking is subjective.

But none of these writers developed the implications of these ideas in the persistent manner of Ockham. In points where the theory of knowledge touches theology Peter Aureol followed Augustine.

III

Ockham's popular fame rests upon the celebrated razor. It is continually at hand throughout his works. 'To employ a number of principles when it is possible to use a few is a waste of time.' 'We must never assume a number of elements unless we are forced to do so.' To work with more entities where it is possible to work with fewer is futile. 'Frustra fit per plura quod potest fieri per paucoria.'[2] The rule is invoked against the excessive verbal divisions which filled the writings of contemporary logicians. At the same time Ockham is critical of loose language in philosophy. 'Aristotle and Averroës', he complains, 'frequently use terms in a misleading metaphorical and figurative sense.'[3] But the rule of economy in explanation is chiefly directed against every form of Realism, against the tendency he found among the *moderni* to treat terms as metaphysical substances. It is upon the entities of the new realist schools who confused words with things that the razor constantly descends. 'Sufficiunt singularia et ita tales res universales omnino frustra ponuntur.' The pervading note of Ockham's philosophical discussions is the rejection of all facets of Realism. Universals have no existence in reality. They are convenient mental fictions, signs standing for many particulars at once.

Ockham bears witness to the domination of Realism in contemporary thought. He declares that all whom he meets agree in asserting that the entity which is in some way universal actually exists in the individual object.[4] From the immense number of arguments against Realism which fill his logical works we may select the following. There was the extreme type of Realism which

---

[1] Petrus Aureoli (died 1322), Ueberweg-Geyer, *Geschichte der Philosophie*, p. 257.
[2] The maxim is employed by other Oxford Franciscans, for instance, Richard of Middleton and Duns Scotus.
[3] Summulae i. 13; Tornay, p. 41.
[4] Sent. i, dist. 2, qu. 7; Tornay, p. 126.

asserted that the universal exists as a mode of being distinct from the individual instance which exemplifies it. Echoing a criticism which we have heard levelled by Abaelard against William of Champeaux, Ockham protests that there is no single identical and simple entity which is present in each of a number of particular things at the same moment. On this view the particular thing and the universal are two distinct existences; and a single thing cannot exist in several other things. But some philosophers offered another interpretation of the universal. They maintained that the universal was capable of being *communicated* to many things at the same time. What is the nature of this communication? If it means that the universal is imparted to many things at once without causing any alteration in itself or multiplying itself in the things, it remains a single identity or an individual; and our former difficulty returns.

We have noticed that it was a cardinal doctrine of Scholastic thought that universals were the essences of things. Duns Scotus had recently given a peculiar turn to this principle. He argued that the universal is not the whole of the essence of an individual but part of its essence. If it were the whole essence the individual thing or person would be the universal. Nevertheless, formal distinctions made by reason in the thing have status in the thing. They are *formalitates*. Ockham replies that even to say that the universals or *formalitates* are part of the essence of an individual implies that in any individual there would be as many distinct objects as there are universals which could be predicated of it.[1] If the universal 'humanity' were an entity distinct from a particular individual and at the same time part of its essence, it would be in a number of different places at the same time. And, what is worse, it would be Judas and Christ simultaneously.

Similar objections are pressed against a further theory proposed by the subtle doctor. The universal, according to him, is not actually different from the individual. It is present in particular things in a contracted form. Humanity is present in Socrates in a specific way. Once more Ockham points out that it would follow that there would be as many universals as there are individuals. And this would mean the denial of universals; there would be no common nature.[2]

Most of Ockham's criticisms against universals are variations on the theme that a single distinct entity appearing in a multiplicity

[1] Sent. i, dist. 2, qu. 4; Tornay, pp. 126–7.   [2] Ib.; Tornay, pp. 127–8.

of individual things is a contradiction in terms. For the universal is described in language proper to the individual. But if it is an individual it is incomprehensible how it can appear in a multitude of individuals. If it is present in a number of particulars it cannot be a single entity. He roundly concludes that there is no such being as a universal in the sense of an entity present in each of a number of items of experiences and common to them. It is as great an impossibility that anything should exist outside the mind in any universal form as it is that a man should at the same time be an ass. To say that the universal has objective being is like saying that the word 'man' is part of the individual to which it refers.[1] Realism is denied, as we shall notice, even to the divine mind. The acceptance of universal realities, apart from the confusions to which it leads, violates the Law of Economy. Knowledge can be described without introducing such types of existence. Universals are unnecessary.

Ockham uncompromisely rejects all modes of Realism. We turn with interest to his own view of knowledge; for we are at a crisis in the history of European thought. It is here that there occurs most markedly the breach with the magnanimous tradition of *philosophia perennis*.

The basis of experience is provided by *notitia intuitiva*, intuition. It alone gives clearness and conviction. The other main division of knowledge, abstract knowledge, gives in comparison doubtful and confused information. Confusion arises when the mind fails to distinguish accurately between items of experience. Whether an object is part of another object, all distinctions in fact, can ultimately be decided only by direct perception. All knowledge of the elements of which terms or objects are composed is derived from this intuition, and the mind can fail to attain truth only when it cannot reach the objects of intuition or when intuition suffers some obstruction. Now the objects of intuition are in the first place individual things. They are not essences or quiddities, but the objects of sense-perception, each of which may differ as much from another as an individual person differs from another person. But intuition is not only of individual objects in the sensible world. It also perceives immediately the relations between objects. When anyone sees Socrates and white at the same time, he is certain that Socrates is white.[2] But before we refer to further elements

---

[1] Sent. i, dist. 2, qu. 7; Abbagnano, p. 88 n.
[2] Sent. i, dist. 2, qu. 7, and ib. Prol. qu. 1; fornay, p. 120.

revealed by intuition we must draw attention to the most important evidence which it provides. Intuition gives knowledge of
reality. It informs us whether an object exists or does not exist.
'Notitia intuitiva rei est talis notitia virtute cujus potest sciri
utrum res sit vel non.'[1] Reality is most securely known in
immediate present experience. Intuitive knowledge is then said
to be perfect. It is imperfect when it passes judgement on past
experience. For even memory images are classified as abstract in
this strict empiricism. When I see a wall or touch a flame, I know
certainly that the wall or flame exists. But if I recall them or
imagine them I am not sure that they exist.[2]

But intuition is not mere sensation. Within it a sensory and an
intellectual factor are distinguished. Sensation is associated with
appetite, of which it is said to be the cause. But sensation, for
example of sight, is not sufficient to produce awareness of an
object; an 'intellectual' intuition is further required. The function of this factor is to classify the object of our intuition, to
pronounce what it is.[3] The sensory factor tells us *that* the thing
exists, the intellectual factor allows us to recognize it; and any
perception requires both elements. This doctrine that *intellectus*
knows sensible things intuitively is a revolution in medieval
ways of thought. That the intellect or understanding could not
know particular sensible things was a cardinal point of Scholastic
teaching. Even for St. Thomas our minds can grasp no more than
the abstract nature of each individual object. We cannot seize
its individuality, for this is conditioned by matter. Our knowledge is confined to universals. But for Ockham there are no
universal essences immanent in things. Matter is not the limiting
factor in individuality; it is the individual itself (so far as
it is a sensible object), and it is apprehended as a recognizable
object by the combined activities of intellect and sensation in
intuition.

The world is directly perceived. All theories of representative
knowledge are repudiated. Ideas which are asserted to resemble
the reality of which they are copies assume acquaintance with
that reality. If anyone saw the statue of Hercules without having
any previous knowledge of Hercules, he might take it to represent
Achilles. Ideas or species which convey a similitude of the real

---

[1] Sent. Prol. qu. 1; Abbagnano, p. 58 n.
[2] *De Princip. Theolog.*, ed. Baudry, p. 133.
[3] Quodlib. i, qu. 15; McKeon, ii, p. 368.

world are logically impossible, and the introduction of them offends
against the principle of economy.[1]

In abolishing any idea or other intermediary between experience
and its object Ockham sweeps away at a stroke the *species intelligibilis* of St. Thomas. The account which the Angelic Doctor gives
of knowledge requires, as we have seen, an intermediary between
object and subject that makes possible the passage of thought.
The view rests on the belief that thought is immanent; knowing is
a mode of being, a realization of Form, and when the active intellect
extracts the intelligible species from the phantoms it is expressing
no less the nature of the object than the nature of the subject.
Thomas often speaks of the intelligible species as though it were a
copy or substitute for the object. But he insists that it is not the
species which is known but the object. But if this is the case
Ockham argues that the intelligible species is otiose. The object and
the mind in direct relation are all that it is necessary to postulate.
Moreover, it is impossible to understand how matter which is
presumed to be incapable of causal action on the immaterial mind
can produce the immaterial species.[2]

Experience is simple and direct. But here two interesting qualifi-
cations in Ockham's empiricism must be described. The first
widens the range of objects which can be intuitively perceived; the
second introduces a reservation into the guarantee given by the
act of perception that objects exist. As regards the first point it is
not only objects perceived by means of the external senses which
can be directly known. Actually it is the region of inner experience, comprising acts of will, pleasure, or sorrow, that are most
immediately and convincingly known. Judgements based on
these processes carry greater certainty than any other class of
contingent propositions. In asserting that the experiences of the
self are better known than external objects, Ockham refers to
the authority of St. Augustine, quoting his argument that while
anyone can doubt the delivery of sense perception no one can be
sceptical regarding his own existence.[3]

Some hesitation concerning the existence of objects perceived
by our external senses is here indicated. And this leads to the
second qualification in Ockham's empiricism. For intuitions may
sometimes be clear without giving guarantee of their existence.

[1] Sent. Prol. qu. 9; Tornay, p. 16; Abbagnano, p. 70 n.
[2] Sent. ii, qu. 15; Tornay, p. 4; cf. Sent. i, dist. 3, qu. 2; Abbagnano, p. 72 n.
[3] Sent. Prol. qu. 1; Tornay, p. 121.

In a passage which has a highly modern ring, it is pointed out that we may continue to see a star after it has been destroyed.[1] And God can give an intuition of an object which has no real existence. But in the natural course of things intuitive knowledge is always caused by objects. It is a contradiction that sight should refer to nothing. A chimera cannot be perceived. Puzzles such as those due to after-images are easily solved. If a person looks at the sun and then goes into a dark room he will have an image of the sun before his eyes; but it is not the sun he sees but the 'light impressed on his eyes'.[2]

The final references of truth, then, are the testimonies of the external or internal senses. These alone in Ockham's terms give evident knowledge. But he does not deny that propositions even of the most general character are not immediately apprehended and recognized as true. 'We apprehend not only simple things, but also propositions and demonstrations.'[3] But the 'assent' by which we judge propositions to be true ultimately depends, when analysed, on the evident awareness of individual experiences. This is so, even of propositions which claim to be self-evident, such as the proposition that the whole is greater than the part. They presuppose the apprehension of individual things, though the immediate assent is not to them.[4]

IV

Ockham has categorically rejected all forms of Realism, and grounded knowledge on direct apprehension of individual objects. 'Nihil est in rerum natura extra animam nisi singulare.' What, then, does he conceive to be the nature of universals? The answer will have a profound effect on medieval life and thought. Unfortunately a precise answer to the question is not easy. He expresses views which are not obviously consistent with one another. The position adopted in the *Commentary on the Sentences* differs from the theory which is maintained in the later works. It is reasonable to suppose that when he wrote the *Summa totius logicae*, the *Septem quodlibeta*, and the *Expositio Aurea* he had changed his opinion.[5]

Berkeley, writing from the standpoint of extreme empiricism four

---

[1] Sent. Prol. qu. 1; Tornay, p. 120.
[2] Quod. vi, qu. 6; McKeon, ii, p. 374; Sent. ii, qu. 15; Abbagnano, p. 68 n.
[3] Sent. Prol. qu. 1; Tornay, p. 122.   [4] Quodlib. iv. 17; McKeon, ii, p. 384.
[5] Mr. Tornay attempts to combine the earlier and the later positions into a coherent doctrine, but the texts plainly point to divergent theories. On this point cf. J. R. Weinberg, *The Philosophical Review*, vol. l, no. 5, pp. 523 ff.

hundred years later, recognized that knowledge is concerned with universals. He observed: 'It is I know a point much insisted on that all knowledge and demonstration are about universal notions, to which I fully agree.'[1] Ockham writes that 'properly speaking there is no science of individuals, but of universals.[2] And so far both the fourteenth- and the eighteenth-century empiricists follow Aristotle and the medieval tradition. But Berkeley immediately went on to add that universality does not consist 'in the absolute positive nature or conception of anything, but in the relations it bears to the particulars signified by it; by virtue whereof it is that things, names, or notions being in their own nature particular are rendered universal. . . . The particular triangle . . . doth stand for and represent all rectilinear triangles whatsoever, and is, in that sense universal.' Ockham's interpretation of thought resembles this position but is more satisfactory, both with regard to the empirical basis of experience and to the function of general ideas.

At the outset one fact must be made clear. Ockham rejects extreme Nominalism. The universal concept is not a mere *vox*, an arbitrary and conventional noise. He rejects the position of Roscellinus on the ground that in this case there would be no species or genus at all; and also on the ground that God and any object external to the mind could become universal equally with what is in the mind. In other words, he assumes that some kind of reality attaches to general notions, and insists that they must be distinguished from the particular objects of intuition.

In the *Commentary on the Sentences* he admits as plausible the view which he afterwards adopted, that universals possess actual existence as a quality of the thinking process, as a psychical experience. But he decides against this theory in favour of another principle. This principle is that universals have only logical status. Their function is to enter propositions as predicates, asserting universality of groups of particular subjects. This logical function does not endow universal terms with any real existence. They are 'meanings'. 'There are certain entities which have only logical being. Thus propositions, syllogisms, and similar topics dealt with by logic possess no objective being, but only logical being. Their being consists in being thought, *eorum esse est eorum cognosci*.'[3]

---

[1] *Principles of Human Knowledge* (1710), Introd. 15.
[2] Sent. i, dist. 2, qu. 8; Abbagnano, p. 90 n.
[3] Ib.; Tornay, p. 132.

Universals have a being of this kind. In order to understand the principle it is necessary to touch on some technical terms which occupy important places in Ockham's doctrine. He classifies the contents of thought under the heading of first and second intentions. First intentions or primary experiences are direct intuitions of things, the mental responses to objects. But they also include complex intuitions of truths. There are immediately evident propositions as well as evident perceptions. The main point is that first intentions refer to elements which are not signs of something other than themselves. Second intentions, or secondary concepts, are defined as signs of first intentions. Here the terms do not refer directly to actual things but to features of things abstracted for special investigation. Two important types of such investigation are grammar and logic. At this point another expression of great significance in Ockham's philosophy is introduced, the expression *suppositio*, substitution. Following the current grammatical logic he classifies terms under three types of *suppositio*, namely *simplex*, *materialis*, and *personalis*; and it is in connexion with the first of these forms of substitution that he makes an important innovation. Terms that are material substitutes refer to grammatical symbols, such as 'nouns', 'adjectives'. Terms that are personal substitutes stand for the particular items referred to in a general term; thus the word 'man' is a personal substitute when it stands for individual men. Now, in the current logic terms that are simple substitutes stand for universals; 'man' stands for 'man-in-general'. For Ockham, terms of this class, *suppositiones simplices*, can only refer to 'intentions' of the mind, to concepts. They cannot refer to any realities. 'A substitution is simple when a term is a substitute for a mental concept. . . . Hence the error of those who believed that there was something in reality besides the singular entity and who held that humanity distinguished from singular instances is something that exists in individuals and is related to their essence.'[1] In all this Ockham is drawing attention to the difference between real meaning and logical meaning, between assertions about forms of discourse and assertions about things. He is distinguishing discussions about what actually exists from discussions about the rational operations which are used in the first type of discourse. Terms of second intention are formal. To confuse them with realities which are individual things

[1] Sum. tot. log. i. 66; Prantl, iii, p. 351, n. 796. Cf. ib. i. 64; Abbagnano, p. 128.

is to abolish the distinction between logic and science. In knowledge about reality, *scientia realis*, the propositions stand for things;
in rational knowledge they stand for mental constructions. The
fatal error is to mix forms of thought with the things thought of,
signs with what they signify. Thus the Aristotelian categories do
not refer to things but to concepts of second intention. There is
nothing actually outside the mind but particular things.

The same point is driven home in a passage in the *Commentary
on the Sentences*. Let us take the proposition *homo est risibilis*.
When this sentence is uttered we hear it, and we hear it with our
bodily ears just as we also perceive colour or light with our
bodily eyes. Accordingly there exist true propositions which are
composed of words or sounds, and concerning which we have some
knowledge. But our knowledge, which is represented by the
spoken propositions, is sometimes a knowledge of reality, sometimes a logical knowledge, although in both cases only words are
given. In the first instance the words stand for certain real things
outside the mind; it is then a question of knowledge of reality. In
the second instance the words represent, not real things, but only
ideas; then it is a question of logical knowledge. But whether their
contents are real or only logical, these propositions always consist of
words. They belong to different branches of knowledge only for this
reason, that some signify objects, while others signify ideas only.[1]

Universals then are second intentions of the simple order. They
refer to terms, not things. 'The secondary process produces the
universals and second intentions and does not presuppose them.'[2]
Universals are signs, standing for a set of qualities or objects; they
are universal by meaning. Thus the historic controversy over the
nature of universals becomes pointless. For to discuss whether a
universal is related to an individual is like discussing whether the
name or sign 'table' is part of the table. Some signs stand for one
thing, others stand for many things, and these are universals; but
everything which actually exists is a single thing. All the difficulties about universals spring from the attempt to make them both
singular and plural at the same time. Species and genus do not
name substances, but signs.

How disturbing these principles were to the traditional beliefs
can be illustrated by Ockham's application of them to theology;
and when we read the passages in the first book of the *Commentary
on the Sentences* in which he criticizes the historic conceptions we

[1] Sent. i, dist. 2, qu. 4.   [2] Sent. ii, qu. 25; Tornay, p. 124.

can understand the charges of heresy which kept him prisoner
at Avignon. For St. Augustine and the realists formless matter
becomes an individual thing, a rock or a tree, in virtue of its participation in an idea, and ideas subsist in the mind of God. Ockham
rejects this view completely. An idea is not a thing; it is a logical
entity, *habet tantum quid nominis.* Ideas cannot therefore constitute part of the divine being. They are rather ideals according to
which God creates individual things, and an ideal can be entertained
only by acquaintance with actual instances which suggest it. A
builder keeps a house before his eyes in order to make another
similar to it. Exemplary ideas, then, arise from acquaintance with
singular things. There are no ideas of genera or essences. When it
is maintained that God knows by means of ideas, the only acceptable sense is that He knows the infinite number of particular
things which are created by Him. This knowledge is particular, not
general. If Plato said that ideas referred to the species and not to
singular objects he was wrong.[1]

Thus the *universale ante rem* is discarded and the divine Ideas are
described as God's creative knowledge of particular things. The
interpretation moves away from the ancient assumptions which
conceived reality in terms of immutable patterns and eternal
reasons. It points to the productive will of God as the ground of
the universe, rather than to His unchangeable essence.

In his later works Ockham, as we have noticed, changes his
position concerning the nature of universals. He adheres to the
main point that they are signs standing for groups of things. But
instead of conceiving them as logical contents formed by the mind
he maintains that they are qualities or aspects of the mind itself.
They inform the mind as white informs a wall.[2] The assumption of
logical fictions interposed between mind and the real objects known
in intuition offends against the Law of Economy.[3] Second intentions no less than first intentions are acts of the mind; they are
real beings or qualities existing in the mind.[4] The process is
described as follows. There is first the direct apprehension of
single things in intuition; the mind then produces an *intentio*
or *passio* which refers to these objects and can stand for them.
These concepts are quite general. Just as the word 'man' no

---

[1] Sent. i, dist. 35, qu. 5; Tornay, p. 137 f.
[2] Expos. Aur. Lib. Perierm. Proem. Abbagnano, p. 92 n.
[3] Quòdlib. iv. 19; McKeon, p. 389.
[4] Ib., pp. 390, 391; cf. Summ. tot. log. i. 12; Abbagnano, p. 93 n.

more signifies Socrates than Plato, so the concept is equally general. Accordingly, concepts or affections (*passiones*) of the mind are natural substitutes for the things themselves, just as words are artificial substitutes.[1]

An interesting distinction is here drawn between universals in the sense of natural expressions of the mind and in the sense of conventional expressions. The latter are words. The former are spontaneous expressions of the mind's relationship with things. Animals and men emit sounds in order to express their feelings; a groan signifies the pain of a sick man, a smile indicates inner joy. In the same way the mind utters expressions which are symbols of groups or patterns of things. These spontaneous mental universals have no external reality.[2] They are mental signs, essential features of the mind's activity.

Ockham does not pursue this theory of natural mental language, *representative* response to the world underlying artificial speech. If pressed further I imagine he would say that natural intentions are ultimately forms of behaviour. He complicates and indeed confuses the theory by frequently speaking of *intentiones* as likenesses of a thing, *similitudines rei*. Such phrases suggest a uniformity of nature between mental concepts and the objects which they represent. What is plain is that the similarity which is predicated of things and in virtue of which the mind is able to express mental concepts and verbal signs standing for groups of objects does not imply any reality beyond distinct similar things. There is no whiteness, only different white things.[3] Mental signs cannot then resemble general entities, for there are none such. In any case it is difficult to see how a process of mind can be like a thing. The phrase, *similitudo rei*, cannot mean any concession to Realism to which Ockham is unequivocally opposed.

V

We can now attempt to assess the Nominalism of William of Ockham; and in order to do so we must glance at some of the philosophical premises on which it rests. The conception of knowledge, of which a rough summary has been given, presumes an outlook on the world which breaks with the main tradition of scholastic thought. Its ancestry lies rather with Stoicism than

[1] Expos. Aur. Lib. Perierm. Abbagnano, p. 94 n.
[2] Sum. tot. log. i. 14; Tornay, p. 125.
[3] Sent. i, dist. 30, qu. 1; Abbagnano, p. 98 n.

with Plato and Aristotle. Since there are no common natures in things, existence is composed of individual items in various relations. Everything that is is an individual thing. In Ockham's language *ens* and *unum*, being and one, are identical. To be one is to be a substance; and to be a substance is to exist.

'It must be maintained undoubtedly that anything imaginable whatsoever, which subsists by itself, is without any addition to it a singular thing and one in number, so that no imaginable thing is singular through having something added to it, but this (i.e. being singular) is an attribute belonging immediately to everything, because everything is *per se* identical with or diverse from others.'[1]

We have seen that for St. Thomas essence is what the object really is. It is its universal nature expressed in its definition. An essence or quiddity can be understood without anything being known of its existence. Existence is a function of matter, by which the essences of composite things are multiplied in numerous individuals. But for Ockham there are no universal essences which require to be expressed in matter in order to become individuals. This is what he means by saying that the singular thing is singular without any addition to it. The singular thing requires no metaphysical 'principle of individuation'. And with the rejection of these distinctions the distinction between essence and existence, which occupies so vital a place in the philosophy and theology of St. Thomas, is abandoned.[2] The refusal to accept formal properties as realities affects the view of matter in other respects. The theory of primary matter had descended from Greek speculation through St. Augustine. The theory had sought to provide for the continuity and connexion of things in their material aspect, and also to supply a passive medium or context for the generation of things by form. As the universal amorphous medium in which definite substances were shaped by forms, it had been conceived as pure potentiality. This notion of a pure potentiality, possessing no actuality nor form, had been severely criticized in the thirteenth century, particularly at Oxford; and Ockham carries forward the criticism. He allows certain common features in all matter, such as its plastic adaptability to many types of substantial forms. But these features have no existence apart from particular things. Primary matter is always *in actu*; or, to speak more accurately, it always has some actuality and embodiment. And these embodi-

---

[1] Expos. Aur. i, Moody, p. 79.
[2] Sum. tot. log. iii. 2, 27; Abbagnano, p. 158 n.

ments are all uniquely different. 'In all generated and existing things the various primary matters are each distinct and different, just as various white objects are different. My primary matter is different from your primary matter.'[1] The positivist and phenomenal tendency of this philosophy is here apparent. In one passage Ockham's thought becomes even more prophetic, for he identifies matter with quantitative dimension. 'It is impossible to have first matter without extension, for matter cannot exist without having parts distant from part. But this amounts to asserting that matter is extended, quantitative and has dimensions.'[2]

The sense of dissatisfaction with the accepted principles of explanation is apparent in a further passage in the *Summulae* where he writes, 'And if it is asked why matter is potentiality and form act, the answer is that such is the nature of the thing, and there is no other cause for it, but that matter is matter and form is form.' This, in truth, is no proper cause, he adds; but we do not know any others.[3]

Other discussions on causation strikingly press the new empirical approach to knowledge. Ockham insists on the empirical origin of our knowledge of causal connexion, dismissing the orthodox belief in formal principles that control the connexion. He maintains that the notion of one particular object is never the sufficient cause of the notion of another particular object.[4] Causal connexion cannot be demonstrated. We find fire and burning present together, but we cannot assume that the burning is due to the fire. It may be due to God, who could produce other effects if He so willed.[5]

Substance, too, becomes unknowable. When we see a fire we know that it is fire; yet in reality we do not know fire in itself but only the accidents of fire, such as its heat.[6] A substance is understood only by negative descriptions, such as 'an entity which subsists by itself', 'an entity underlying all accidents'.[7] The position reminds us of Locke's 'supposition one knows not what support of such qualities which are capable of producing simple ideas in us; which qualities are commonly called accidents'.[8] The ancient doctrines concerning the mind are also challenged.

[1] Summulae i. 18 and i. 14; Tornay, p. 35, nn. 16 and 17.
[2] Summulae i. 14; Tornay, p. 36.
[3] Summulae i. 23; Tornay, p. 38.
[4] Sent. Prol. qu. 9; Abbagnano, p. 167 n.
[5] Sent. ii, qu. 5; Tornay, p. 69.
[6] Sent. i, dist. 3, qu. 2; Abbagnano, p. 162 n.
[7] Ib., dist. 3, qu. 2; Tornay, p. 59.   [8] Essay, bk. ii, ch. 23.

'Our understanding of the intellectual soul as an immaterial and incorruptible form which is totally in the whole and totally in every part cannot be accepted as evident from either reason or experience. We cannot know whether such form is in us, or that it is the nature of such substance in us to be intellectual, or that the soul is the form of the body. I do not care how Aristotle felt about this, because everywhere he himself appears on this point to be uncertain. We hold the three foregoing propositions only by faith.'[1]

In fine, he moves away at every point from the historic meta-physical interpretations of experience. Since there are no universal principles in things, principles are generalizations from particulars. His preference for particular sensible realities over metaphysical entities governs his contributions to physics. His observations on movement provide examples of this method. The accepted way of interpreting movement was to understand it as the realization of a Form. Ockham asserts that the moving body is the motion. There is no being inherent in bodies which is movement; there are simply the moving bodies which we perceive.[2] The characteristic note is struck again in the discussions on the nature of time. 'Time is not a latent unknowable thing.'[3] It is the measure of bodies in motion, the ultimate reference being the fixed stars. Such hints encouraged a profound revolution in the set of ideas which had descended from classical Greek thought. They were taken up by the school of Parisian Nominalists who followed Ockham, men such as John Buridan, Nicholas of Oresme, and Marsilius of Inghen. These Nominalist philosophers made important advances in physical theory. William of Ockham's influence on the birth of science is undoubted.

VI

But it was in the fields of philosophy and of theology that his views produced their most disturbing effects. Throughout the whole period of medieval thought the relation between the provinces of reason and revealed Faith had constantly occupied the attention of philosophers. The problem is present at every point of their work. Some authorities at each period completely severed rational inquiry from the traditional content of Revela-tion, in the interest of the former. The dogmas of the Faith are sufficient, and the exercise of rational inquiry beyond what is

---

[1] Summulae i. 14; Abbagnano, p. 179 n.
[2] Sent. ii, qu. 26; Tornay, p. 39.　　　　[3] Summulae iv. 3; Tornay, p. 43.

necessary in order to accept them is unnecessary and dangerous.
St. Bernard and Peter Damian are, in different ways, instances of
this unspeculative piety. But the typical attitude of the masters
of medieval thought is *Fides quaerens intellectum*. This is the
programme of Augustine, of Anselm, of Thomas Aquinas. It is
the task of reason to clarify in logical terms, as far as possible, the
deliverances of Revelation. It is impossible that Christian beliefs
should be unreasonable; and the whole aim of the *Summa Contra
Gentiles* is to show how nearly human inquiry can approach to the
teaching of theology. But Thomas went farther than his predecessors in allowing to the science of temporal things a free scope
independent of theology. His definition of the provinces of Faith
and Reason was provoked by the influence of Averroës who had
argued that reason is incompetent in theological matters. But now,
in the face of the work of Thomas, the sceptical teaching of Averroës was forcibly revived. Ockham denies that any of the central
beliefs of religion can be logically demonstrated. He finds the argument which St. Thomas had elaborated in *Summa Contra Gentiles*
inconclusive. Thomas had argued, after Aristotle, that movement
entails an external agent which initiates the movement. If we are
to avoid an infinite regress we are obliged to postulate a First
Mover. Ockham replies that it is reasonable to hold that some
things move themselves without the intervention of another agent.
He adduces as instances not only the mind and the angels, but also
weight (*gravitas*).[1] Nor does he accept the point that an infinite
regress in the series of movers is a logical impossibility. On the
contrary, an infinite regress is a plain fact in certain cases. For
example, if a continuous surface is struck at one end motion is
produced in the adjacent part; that part moves the next, and so on
to infinity.[1] Ockham is willing to admit that Thomas's conclusion
that there is an unmoved mover is a more probable position than
its opposite; but he refuses to allow that it is proved by his
arguments.

Even the belief in one God is shown to be not susceptible of
demonstration. And a similar attitude is taken concerning the
doctrine of the infinity of God. In a word, conclusive philosophical knowledge of God cannot be attained. Our concepts of Him
suffer the defect of all concepts; they cannot establish existence.
In order to know God as an existent being we should have to
apprehend Him in intuition; and this is impossible.

[1] Cent. Theolog. i; Tornay, p. 190.

Scholasticism was inspired by the belief in the rational unity of philosophy and theology. In the schools of Paris and Oxford it now began to be openly asserted that Christian dogmas could not be supported by reasonable proof; natural reason could show them at the best to be probable inferences. At the worst, when philosophic argument led to the opposite conclusion, the believer was invited to embrace by Faith what his reason rejected. Masters became ready, both in disputations in the schools and in their treatises on the *Sentences*, to defend theories contrary to theological doctrine. These opinions were often put forward under the guise of dialectical exercises. In his work *On the Power of Emperors and Popes* Ockham excuses his heretical utterances by remarking that Catholics can be seen denying points of faith by way of exercise without incurring reproach.[1] But this outlook was a precarious one that heralded deep fissures in medieval culture. Many religious minds turned away from the dialectical theology of the schools towards a practical and devotional rule founded on the simple teaching of the Gospels. Such was Gerard Groote's ideal expressed in the Brotherhood of the Common Life at Deventer. The more speculative returned to the allegorical riches of Neoplatonism. Even during the lifetime of Ockham three great mystical writers— Eckhart, Suso, and Ruysbroeck—had expressed this form of the reaction against theological metaphysics. The agnosticism of Ockham contributed towards the theological pessimism characteristic of the last period of the Middle Ages. And when Luther struck his blow against the edifice of Catholic belief he hailed Ockham as his master.

VII

But our concern here is with the more strictly philosophical outcome of Nominalism. The successors of Ockham developed his sceptical treatment of knowledge. It was argued that we can be sure only of sensations and of the existence of our minds. Now began the repudiation of Aristotle which attained such extravagant heights in the following century. One of Ockham's disciples, Nicholas of Autrecourt, observed that 'in all his natural philosophy and metaphysics Aristotle has hardly reached two evidently certain conclusions, perhaps not even a single one'. And another Nominalist, Peter d'Ailly, asserted that Aristotle's doctrine merits the name of opinion rather than of knowledge. It is true that the

---

[1] Op. cit. iii.

writings of Nicholas were condemned; but Peter d'Ailly became a cardinal. The teaching of Ockham was condemned four times at Paris between 1339 and 1347. Yet it became ascendant everywhere in Europe. The obscure positive movement in this general repudiation of the standard authorities was the search for a new criterion of evidence. But Ockham's conception of thought had severed the general and formal elements from immediate appre- hension. The principle that the universals which constitute the content of thought are terms which stand for cross-sections of individual things introduced a division in the schools which marked out two directions for the subsequent philosophy of knowledge. On the one hand, the formal treatment of terms in propositions produced an elaborate technique of symbolic logic. On the other, the narrowness of the field within which Ockham had confined certain knowledge of reality developed into a sub- jective empiricism. But later philosophers were confronted not only with the task of surmounting the abstractions of Nomina- lism. They were led by the general advance in scientific method to broaden the Scholastic conception of Realism. The universal in thought was perceived to include not only class notions, but to embrace other forms of essential connexions. Yet in the course of modern inquiry into the principles of knowledge Nominalism as well as Realism has been revived in terms which recall the great conflicts of the Middle Ages.

In particular, English philosophy has been dominated by Nominalist theories. Hobbes, Locke, Berkeley, Hume, Hamilton, and Mill express views on the nature of general ideas which are parallel to those of Ockham. Mill, for instance, maintains that 'we think by means of concrete phenomena, such as are presented in experience or represented in imagination, and by means of names, which being in a peculiar manner associated with certain elements of the concrete images arrest our attention on those elements'.[1] In contemporary discussion there is wide concentration on the rela- tion of thought to language, and the work of these schools has brought about a revival of Nominalism. On the other hand, Realism has been a central note in other modern systems of thought. The debt of Descartes to Scholastic principles has been traced by Professor Gilson. And since the seventeenth century Realism has been asserted in many forms, notably by Hegel and his disciples in Germany, Italy, and England. And there are

[1] *Examination of Sir William Hamilton's Philosophy*, p. 330.

numbers of Realists among philosophers in our own day, some
of whom (such as those belonging to the school of Husserl)
acknowledge their obligation to their medieval predecessors. And
in many discussions besides those concerned with the theory of
knowledge the old issues are perpetually reappearing. Extreme
Realism is maintained by numerous writers who investigate the
nature of Goodness or of Beauty, who uphold the corporate
character of the Church, or who press the claims of Nationality
or Labour or the State. Nominalism is advocated by others in the
name of individuality and democracy.[1]

The secular and scientific roots of modern speculation have
transformed the problem. But it remains a vital issue. It seems
reasonable to suppose that brownness or generosity or man refer to
identities which are common to many different particular things.
On the other hand, it appears equally clear that such characters
are in each instance as particular as the particular things which
they qualify. The brownness of curtains and tables and dresses is
in each case distinct and separate; and even when it looks the same
it is distinct in its various instances. If we pursue the question we
are confronted on the one hand with the problem of the relation of
a thing to its qualities, the problem of substance; on the other hand
with the question of the status in reality of the abstract unities
which thought and science apprehend. If Nominalist theories
are to be accepted we must believe that the common principles
sought for in particular things are fictions. But to abolish the
objectivity of universals in *some* sense is to abolish, as St. Thomas
would say, the possibility of exploring the nature of anything. He
insisted that universals have their foundations in objects and so
far are indisputably real. All thinking, he maintained, presupposes
certain irreducible modes of unity, and these are not psychical
patterns contributed by subjects but essential features of objects.
But the exploration of the universal nature by means of general
terms does not imply the self-subsistent entities, man-in-general
or colour-as-such upon which the medieval and eighteenth-century

---

[1] Here is a surprising incursion of the debate into the field of law. 'It may seem
a bold and reckless statement to assert that an adequate discussion of cases like
Berry v. *Donovan*, *Adair* v. *United States*, or *Commonwealth* v. *Boston and Maine R.*
involves the whole medieval controversy over the reality of universals. And yet,
the confident assertion of "immutable principles of justice inhering in the very idea
of free government" made by the writers of these decisions, and the equally
confident assertion of their critics that there are no such principles, show how
impossible it is to keep out of metaphysics.' Morris R. Cohen, *Harvard Law
Review*, xxix, p. 628.

Nominalists poured their scorn. What is sought are systems which are intrinsic to the nature of things.

The issue cannot be further argued here. Our purpose in these brief accounts of medieval views on knowledge has been expository rather than critical. We have attempted no more than to indicate some of the questions relating to knowledge which occupied the schools, and to exhibit the way in which they were discussed by representative thinkers. In the philosophical passages of St. Augustine we have watched the rise of that enduring impulse in Christian reflection which is preoccupied with indestructible truth and the eternal reasons. We have followed the first great assault on the high Realism that had descended from Augustine to the Cathedral schools of the eleventh century. In the philosophy of St. Thomas we have witnessed, so far as a slight sketch allows, a comprehensive and subtle endeavour to combine the general and particular, the sensible and the intellectual, elements of experience into an harmonious scheme on Aristotelian lines. Finally, we have briefly surveyed the critical challenge to the assumptions of the main tradition of Christian metaphysics that appeared in the fourteenth century. The scepticism that was encouraged by the searching inquiries of Ockham and the Terminists into the bases of knowledge, contributed to the disruption of society in the fifteenth century. From that disruption there grew fresh principles of truth and new formulations of the ancient problems of the Realists and Nominalists. But even here the great schoolmen can stimulate and instruct us. And without acquaintance with their methods and opinions we lose sense of the continuity of European thought.

BIBLIOGRAPHY

General works on Medieval Philosophy:

E. BRÉHIER, *La Philosophie du Moyen Âge.* Paris, 1937.

E. GILSON, *La Philosophie au Moyen Âge.* Paris, 1922.

—— *L'Esprit de la philosophie mediévale.* 2 vols., Paris, 1932.

—— und C. BÖHNER, *Die Geschichte der christlichen Philosophie.* Paderborn, 1939.

R. McKEON, *Selections from Medieval Philosophers.* 2 vols., London, 1930.

F. UEBERWEG, *Grundriss der Geschichte der Philosophie,* Vol. II, *Die patristische und scholastische Philosophie,* 11th edition, edited by B. Geyer. Berlin, 1928.

M. DE WULF, *Histoire de la philosophie mediévale.* Louvain, 1924.

St. Augustine:

C. BOYER, *Essais sur la doctrine de St. Augustin.* Paris, 1932.

E. GILSON, *Introduction à l'étude de Saint Augustin.* Paris, 1929.

H. I. MARROU, *Saint Augustin et la fin de la culture antique.* Paris, 1938.

H. POPE, *Saint Augustine of Hippo.* London, 1937.

E. PRZYWARA, *An Augustine Synthesis.* London, 1936.

Various, *A monument to St. Augustine.* London, 1930.

Abaelard:

E. GILSON, *The Unity of Philosophical Experience.* London, 1938. (Chapter I.)

C. DE RÉMUSAT, *Abélard, sa vie, sa philosophie et sa théologie.* 2 vols., Paris, 1855.

T. G. SIKES, *Peter Abailard.* London, 1932.

St. Thomas Aquinas:

M. C. D'ARCY, *Thomas Aquinas.* London, 1934.

E. GILSON, *The Philosophy of St. Thomas Aquinas,* translated by E. Bullough. London, 1937.

G. RABEAU, *Species, Verbum.* Paris, 1938.

P. ROUSSELOT, *L'intellectualisme de Saint Thomas.* 2nd ed., Paris, 1924.

A. D. SERTILLANGES, *Saint Thomas d'Aquin.* 2 vols., Paris, 1910.

—— *Foundations of Thomistic Philosophy,* translated by G. Anstruther. London, 1931.

William of Ockham:

N. ABBAGNANO, *Guglielmo di Ockham.* Lanciano, 1931.

E. GILSON, *The Unity of Philosophical Experience.* London, 1938. (Chapter III.)

E. A. MOODY, *The Logic of William of Ockham.* London, 1935.

G. PRANTL, *Geschichte der Logik im Abendlande.* Leipzig, 1867. (Vol. III, Chap. 19.)

S. C. TORNAY, *Ockham, Studies and Selections.* La Salle, Illinois, 1938.

INDEX

PRINTED IN GREAT BRITAIN AT THE UNIVERSITY PRESS, OXFORD
BY VIVIAN RIDLER, PRINTER TO THE UNIVERSITY